PENGUIN MODERN CLASSICS

Howl, Kaddish and Other Poems

Allen Ginsberg was born in Newark, New Jersey in 1926. As a Columbia College student in the 1940s he began close friendships with William S. Burroughs and Jack Kerouac, forming the core of the Beat Generation, and, while living in California in the mid 1950s, befriended, among others, San Francisco Renaissance poets Gary Snyder and Michael McClure. It was in California, in 1956, that he published his first volume, *Howl and Other Poems*. 'Howl' overcame censorship trials to become one of the most widely read poems of the century. A member of the American Academy of Arts and Letters, Allen Ginsberg was awarded the medal of Chevalier de l'Ordre des Arts et Lettres by the French Minister of Culture in 1993, honoured as Harvard Phi Beta Kappa Poet 1994 and co-founded the Jack Kerouac School of Disembodied Poetics at the Naropa Institute, the first Accredited Buddhist college in the western world. Ginsberg died in New York, where he lived for most of his life, on 5 April 1997. He continued to write until the last few days of his life and died surrounded by his friends and family. His publications include the annotated *Howl*, *White Shroud: Poems 1980–1985*, *Cosmopolitan Greetings*, *Journals Mid-Fifties: 1954–1958*, *Collected Poems 1947–1995*. Rhino Records released his four-CD box *Holy Soul Jelly Roll: Poems & Songs 1949–1993*.

ALLEN GINSBERG

Howl, Kaddish and Other Poems

PENGUIN BOOKS

PENGUIN CLASSICS

Published by the Penguin Group
Penguin Books Ltd, 80 Strand, London WC2R ORL, England
Penguin Group (USA) Inc., 375 Hudson Street, New York, New York 10014, USA
Penguin Group (Canada), 90 Eglinton Avenue East, Suite 700, Toronto, Ontario, Canada M4P 2Y3
(a division of Pearson Penguin Canada Inc.)
Penguin Ireland, 25 St Stephen's Green, Dublin 2, Ireland (a division of Penguin Books Ltd)
Penguin Group (Australia), 250 Camberwell Road, Camberwell, Victoria 3124, Australia
(a division of Pearson Australia Group Pty Ltd)
Penguin Books India Pvt Ltd, 11 Community Centre, Panchsheel Park,
New Delhi – 110 017, India
Penguin Group (NZ), 67 Apollo Drive, Rosedale, North Shore 0632, New Zealand
(a division of Pearson New Zealand Ltd)
Penguin Books (South Africa) (Pty) Ltd, 24 Sturdee Avenue,
Rosebank, Johannesburg 2196, South Africa

Penguin Books Ltd, Registered Offices: 80 Strand, London WC2R ORL, England

www.penguin.com

Howl and Other Poems first published 1956
Kaddish and Other Poems first published 1961
Published in this joint edition in Penguin Classics 2009

4

Copyright © Allen Ginsberg, 1956, 1961
All rights reserved

Set in 10.5/13pt Dante MT
Typeset by Palimpsest Book Production Limited, Grangemouth, Stirlingshire
Printed in England by Clays Ltd, St Ives plc

978-0-141-19016-7

www.greenpenguin.co.uk

Penguin Books is committed to a sustainable future
for our business, our readers and our planet.
The book in your hands is made from paper
certified by the Forest Stewardship Council.

Contents

Contents

'Howl' for Carl Solomon

When he was younger, and I was younger, I used to know Allen Ginsberg, a young poet living in Paterson, New Jersey, where he, son of a well-known poet, had been born and grew up. He was physically slight of build and mentally much disturbed by the life which he had encountered about him during those first years after the First World War as it was exhibited to him in and about New York City. He was always on the point of 'going away', where it didn't seem to matter; he disturbed me, I never thought he'd live to grow up and write a book of poems. His ability to survive, travel, and go on writing astonishes me. That he has gone on developing and perfecting his art is no less amazing to me.

Now he turns up fifteen or twenty years later with an arresting poem. Literally he has, from all the evidence, been through hell. On the way he met a man named Carl Solomon with whom he shared among the teeth and excrement of this life something that cannot be described but in the words he has used to describe it. It is a howl of defeat. Not defeat at all for he has gone through defeat as if it were an ordinary experience, a trivial experience. Everyone in this life is defeated but a man, if he be a man, is not defeated.

It is the poet, Allen Ginsberg, who has gone, in his own body, through the horrifying experiences described from life in these pages. The wonder of the thing is not that he has survived but that he, from the very depths, has found a fellow whom he can love, a love he celebrates without looking aside in these poems. Say what you will, he proves to us, in spite of the most debasing experiences that life can offer a man, the spirit of love survives to ennoble our lives if we have the wit and the courage and the faith – and the art! to persist.

It is the belief in the art of poetry that has gone hand in hand with this man into his Golgotha, from that charnel house, similar in every way, to that of the Jews in the past war. But this is in our own country, our own fondest purlieus. We are blind and live our blind lives out in blindness. Poets are damned but they are not blind, they see with the eyes of the angels. This poet sees through and all around the horrors he partakes of in the very intimate details of his poem. He avoids nothing but experiences it to the hilt. He contains it. Claims it as his own – and, we believe, laughs at it and has the time and affrontery to love a fellow of his choice and record that love in a well-made poem. Hold back the edges of your gowns, Ladies, we are going through hell.

William Carlos Williams

Howl

For Carl Solomon

I

I saw the best minds of my generation destroyed by madness,
    starving hysterical naked,
dragging themselves through the negro streets at dawn looking
    for an angry fix,
angelheaded hipsters burning for the ancient heavenly connec-
    tion to the starry dynamo in the machinery of night,
who poverty and tatters and hollow-eyed and high sat up
    smoking in the supernatural darkness of cold-water flats
    floating across the tops of cities contemplating jazz,
who bared their brains to Heaven under the El and saw Moham-
    medan angels staggering on tenement roofs illuminated,
who passed through universities with radiant cool eyes hallu-
    cinating Arkansas and Blake-light tragedy among the
    scholars of war,
who were expelled from the academies for crazy & publishing
    obscene odes on the windows of the skull,
who cowered in unshaven rooms in underwear, burning their
    money in wastebaskets and listening to the Terror
    through the wall,
who got busted in their pubic beards returning through Laredo
    with a belt of marijuana for New York,
who ate fire in paint hotels or drank turpentine in Paradise
    Alley, death, or purgatoried their torsos night after night
with dreams, with drugs, with waking nightmares, alcohol and
    cock and endless balls,

incomparable blind streets of shuddering cloud and light-
    ning in the mind leaping toward poles of Canada &
    Paterson, illuminating all the motionless world of Time
    between,
Peyote solidities of halls, backyard green tree cemetery dawns,
    wine drunkenness over the rooftops, storefront boroughs
    of teahead joyride neon blinking traffic light, sun and
    moon and tree vibrations in the roaring winter dusks
    of Brooklyn, ashcan rantings and kind king light of
    mind,
who chained themselves to subways for the endless ride from
    Battery to holy Bronx on benzedrine until the noise of
    wheels and children brought them down shuddering
    mouth-wracked and battered bleak of brain all drained
    of brilliance in the drear light of Zoo,
who sank all night in submarine light of Bickford's floated
    out and sat through the stale beer afternoon in desolate
    Fugazzi's, listening to the crack of doom on the hydrogen
    jukebox,
who talked continuously seventy hours from park to pad to bar
    to Bellevue to museum to the Brooklyn Bridge,
a lost battalion of platonic conversationalists jumping down
    the stoops off fire escapes off windowsills off Empire
    State out of the moon,
yacketayakking screaming vomiting whispering facts and
    memories and anecdotes and eyeball kicks and shocks of
    hospitals and jails and wars,
whole intellects disgorged in total recall for seven days and
    nights with brilliant eyes, meat for the Synagogue cast
    on the pavement,
who vanished into nowhere Zen New Jersey leaving a trail of
    ambiguous picture postcards of Atlantic City Hall,
suffering Eastern sweats and Tangerian bone-grindings and
    migraines of China under junk-withdrawal in Newark's
    bleak furnished room,
who wandered around and around at midnight in the railroad

yard wondering where to go, and went, leaving no
    broken hearts,

who lit cigarettes in boxcars boxcars boxcars racketing through
    snow toward lonesome farms in grandfather night,

who studied Plotinus Poe St John of the Cross telepathy and
    bop kabbalah because the cosmos instinctively vibrated
    at their feet in Kansas,

who loned it through the streets of Idaho seeking visionary
    indian angels who were visionary indian angels,

who thought they were only mad when Baltimore gleamed in
    supernatural ecstasy,

who jumped in limousines with the Chinaman of Oklahoma on
    the impulse of winter midnight streetlight smalltown rain,

who lounged hungry and lonesome through Houston seeking
    jazz or sex or soup, and followed the brilliant Spaniard
    to converse about America and Eternity, a hopeless task,
    and so took ship to Africa,

who disappeared into the volcanoes of Mexico leaving behind
    nothing but the shadow of dungarees and the lava and
    ash of poetry scattered in fireplace Chicago,

who reappeared on the West Coast investigating the F.B.I. in
    beards and shorts with big pacifist eyes sexy in their dark
    skin passing out incomprehensible leaflets,

who burned cigarette holes in their arms protesting the narcotic
    tobacco haze of Capitalism,

who distributed Supercommunist pamphlets in Union Square
    weeping and undressing while the sirens of Los Alamos
    wailed them down, and wailed down Wall, and the Staten
    Island ferry also wailed,

who broke down crying in white gymnasiums naked and trem-
    bling before the machinery of other skeletons,

who bit detectives in the neck and shrieked with delight in
    policecars for committing no crime but their own wild
    cooking pederasty and intoxication,

who howled on their knees in the subway and were dragged off
    the roof waving genitals and manuscripts,

who let themselves be fucked in the ass by saintly motorcyclists,
and screamed with joy,

who blew and were blown by those human seraphim, the sailors,
caresses of Atlantic and Caribbean love,

who balled in the morning in the evenings in rosegardens and
the grass of public parks and cemeteries scattering their
semen freely to whomever come who may,

who hiccuped endlessly trying to giggle but wound up with a
sob behind a partition in a Turkish Bath when the blond
& naked angel came to pierce them with a sword,

who lost their loveboys to the three old shrews of fate the one
eyed shrew of the heterosexual dollar the one eyed shrew
that winks out of the womb and the one eyed shrew that
does nothing but sit on her ass and snip the intellectual
golden threads of the craftsman's loom,

who copulated ecstatic and insatiate with a bottle of beer
a sweetheart a package of cigarettes a candle and fell
off the bed, and continued along the floor and down
the hall and ended fainting on the wall with a vision
of ultimate cunt and come eluding the last gyzym of
consciousness,

who sweetened the snatches of a million girls trembling in the
sunset, and were red eyed in the morning but prepared
to sweeten the snatch of the sunrise, flashing buttocks
under barns and naked in the lake,

who went out whoring through Colorado in myriad stolen
night-cars, N.C., secret hero of these poems, cocksman
and Adonis of Denver—joy to the memory of his innu-
merable lays of girls in empty lots & diner backyards,
moviehouses' rickety rows, on mountaintops in caves or
with gaunt waitresses in familiar roadside lonely petti-
coat upliftings & especially secret gas-station solipsisms
of johns, & hometown alleys too,

who faded out in vast sordid movies, were shifted in dreams,
woke on a sudden Manhattan, and picked themselves up
out of basements hungover with heartless Tokay and

horrors of Third Avenue iron dreams & stumbled to unemployment offices,

who walked all night with their shoes full of blood on the snowbank docks waiting for a door in the East River to open to a room full of steamheat and opium,

who created great suicidal dramas on the apartment cliff-banks of the Hudson under the wartime blue floodlight of the moon & their heads shall be crowned with laurel in oblivion,

who ate the lamb stew of the imagination or digested the crab at the muddy bottom of the rivers of Bowery,

who wept at the romance of the streets with their pushcarts full of onions and bad music,

who sat in boxes breathing in the darkness under the bridge, and rose up to build harpsichords in their lofts,

who coughed on the sixth floor of Harlem crowned with flame under the tubercular sky surrounded by orange crates of theology,

who scribbled all night rocking and rolling over lofty incantations which in the yellow morning were stanzas of gibberish,

who cooked rotten animals lung heart feet tail borsht & tortillas dreaming of the pure vegetable kingdom,

who plunged themselves under meat trucks looking for an egg,

who threw their watches off the roof to cast their ballot for Eternity outside of Time, & alarm clocks fell on their heads every day for the next decade,

who cut their wrists three times successively unsuccessfully, gave up and were forced to open antique stores where they thought they were growing old and cried,

who were burned alive in their innocent flannel suits on Madison Avenue amid blasts of leaden verse & the tanked-up clatter of the iron regiments of fashion & the nitroglycerine shrieks of the fairies of advertising & the mustard gas of sinister intelligent editors, or were run down by the drunken taxicabs of Absolute Reality,

who jumped off the Brooklyn Bridge this actually happened
and walked away unknown and forgotten into the ghostly
daze of Chinatown soup alleyways & firetrucks, not even
one free beer,

who sang out of their windows in despair, fell out of the subway
window, jumped in the filthy Passaic, leaped on negroes,
cried all over the street, danced on broken wineglasses
barefoot smashed phonograph records of nostalgic Euro-
pean 1930s German jazz finished the whiskey and threw
up groaning into the bloody toilet, moans in their ears
and the blast of colossal steam-whistles,

who barreled down the highways of the past journeying to
each other's hotrod-Golgotha jail-solitude watch or
Birmingham jazz incarnation,

who drove crosscountry seventytwo hours to find out if I had
a vision or you had a vision or he had a vision to find out
Eternity,

who journeyed to Denver, who died in Denver, who came back
to Denver & waited in vain, who watched over Denver
& brooded & loned in Denver and finally went away to
find out the Time, & now Denver is lonesome for her
heroes,

who fell on their knees in hopeless cathedrals praying for each
other's salvation and light and breasts, until the soul illu-
minated its hair for a second,

who crashed through their minds in jail waiting for impossible
criminals with golden heads and the charm of reality in
their hearts who sang sweet blues to Alcatraz,

who retired to Mexico to cultivate a habit, or Rocky Mount to
tender Buddha or Tangiers to boys or Southern Pacific to
the black locomotive or Harvard to Narcissus to Wood-
lawn to the daisychain or grave,

who demanded sanity trials accusing the radio of hypnotism
& were left with their insanity & their hands & a hung
jury,

who threw potato salad at CCNY lecturers on Dadaism and

subsequently presented themselves on the granite
steps of the madhouse with shaven heads and harle-
quin speech of suicide, demanding instantaneous
lobotomy,

and who were given instead the concrete void of insulin
Metrazol electricity hydrotherapy psychotherapy occu-
pational therapy pingpong & amnesia,

who in humorless protest overturned only one symbolic ping-
pong table, resting briefly in catatonia,

returning years later truly bald except for a wig of blood, and
tears and fingers, to the visible madman doom of the
wards of the madtowns of the East,

Pilgrim State's Rockland's and Greystone's foetid halls, bick-
ering with the echoes of the soul, rocking and rolling
in the midnight solitude-bench dolmen-realms of love,
dream of life a night-mare, bodies turned to stone as
heavy as the moon,

with mother finally ******, and the last fantastic book flung
out of the tenement window, and the last door closed
at 4 A.M. and the last telephone slammed at the wall in
reply and the last furnished room emptied down to the
last piece of mental furniture, a yellow paper rose twisted
on a wire hanger in the closet, and even that imaginary,
nothing but a hopeful little bit of hallucination—

ah, Carl, while you are not safe I am not safe, and now you're
really in the total animal soup of time—

and who therefore ran through the icy streets obsessed with a
sudden flash of the alchemy of the use of the ellipse the
catalog the meter & the vibrating plane,

who dreamt and made incarnate gaps in Time & Space through
images juxtaposed, and trapped the archangel of the soul
between 2 visual images and joined the elemental verbs
and set the noun and dash of consciousness together
jumping with sensation of Pater Omnipotens Aeterna
Deus

to recreate the syntax and measure of poor human prose and

stand before you speechless and intelligent and shaking with shame, rejected yet confessing out the soul to conform to the rhythm of thought in his naked and endless head,

the madman bum and angel beat in Time, unknown, yet putting down here what might be left to say in time come after death,

and rose reincarnate in the ghostly clothes of jazz in the goldhorn shadow of the band and blew the suffering of America's naked mind for love into an eli eli lamma lamma sabacthani saxophone cry that shivered the cities down to the last radio

with the absolute heart of the poem of life butchered out of their own bodies good to eat a thousand years.

II

What sphinx of cement and aluminum bashed open their skulls and ate up their brains and imagination?

Moloch! Solitude! Filth! Ugliness! Ashcans and unobtainable dollars! Children screaming under the stairways! Boys sobbing in armies! Old men weeping in the parks!

Moloch! Moloch! Nightmare of Moloch! Moloch the loveless! Mental Moloch! Moloch the heavy judger of men!

Moloch the incomprehensible prison! Moloch the crossbone soulless jailhouse and Congress of sorrows! Moloch whose buildings are judgment! Moloch the vast stone of war! Moloch the stunned governments!

Moloch whose mind is pure machinery! Moloch whose blood is running money! Moloch whose fingers are ten armies! Moloch whose breast is a cannibal dynamo! Moloch whose ear is a smoking tomb!

Moloch whose eyes are a thousand blind windows! Moloch whose skyscrapers stand in the long streets like endless Jehovahs! Moloch whose factories dream and croak in the fog! Moloch whose smokestacks and antennae crown the cities!

Moloch whose love is endless oil and stone! Moloch whose soul is electricity and banks! Moloch whose poverty is the specter of genius! Moloch whose fate is a cloud of sexless hydrogen! Moloch whose name is the Mind!

Moloch in whom I sit lonely! Moloch in whom I dream Angels! Crazy in Moloch! Cocksucker in Moloch! Lacklove and manless in Moloch!

Moloch who entered my soul early! Moloch in whom I am a consciousness without a body! Moloch who frightened me out of my natural ecstasy! Moloch whom I abandon! Wake up in Moloch! Light streaming out of the sky!

Moloch! Moloch! Robot apartments! invisible suburbs! skeleton treasuries! blind capitals! demonic industries! spectral nations! invincible mad houses! granite cocks! monstrous bombs!

They broke their backs lifting Moloch to Heaven! Pavements, trees, radios, tons! lifting the city to Heaven which exists and is everywhere about us!

Visions! omens! hallucinations! miracles! ecstasies! gone down the American river!

Dreams! adorations! illuminations! religions! the whole boatload of sensitive bullshit!

Breakthroughs! over the river! flips and crucifixions! gone down the flood! Highs! Epiphanies! Despairs! Ten years' animal screams and suicides! Minds! New loves! Mad generation! down on the rocks of Time!

Real holy laughter in the river! They saw it all! the wild eyes! the holy yells! They bade farewell! They jumped off the roof! to solitude! waving! carrying flowers! Down to the river! into the street!

III

Carl Solomon! I'm with you in Rockland
>   where you're madder than I am
I'm with you in Rockland
>   where you must feel very strange
I'm with you in Rockland
>   where you imitate the shade of my mother
I'm with you in Rockland
>   where you've murdered your twelve secretaries
I'm with you in Rockland
>   where you laugh at this invisible humor
I'm with you in Rockland
>   where we are great writers on the same dreadful type-
>   writer
I'm with you in Rockland
>   where your condition has become serious and is reported
>   on the radio
I'm with you in Rockland
>   where the faculties of the skull no longer admit the
>   worms of the senses
I'm with you in Rockland
>   where you drink the tea of the breasts of the spinsters of
>   Utica
I'm with you in Rockland
>   where you pun on the bodies of your nurses the harpies
>   of the Bronx
I'm with you in Rockland
>   where you scream in a straightjacket that you're losing
>   the game of the actual pingpong of the abyss
I'm with you in Rockland
>   where you bang on the catatonic piano the soul is inno-
>   cent and immortal it should never die ungodly in an
>   armed madhouse
I'm with you in Rockland
>   where fifty more shocks will never return your soul to its

body again from its pilgrimage to a cross in the void
I'm with you in Rockland
where you accuse your doctors of insanity and plot the
Hebrew socialist revolution against the fascist national
Golgotha
I'm with you in Rockland
where you will split the heavens of Long Island and resur-
rect your living human Jesus from the superhuman tomb
I'm with you in Rockland
where there are twenty-five-thousand mad comrades all
together singing the final stanzas of the Internationale
I'm with you in Rockland
where we hug and kiss the United States under our
bedsheets the United States that coughs all night and
won't let us sleep
I'm with you in Rockland
where we wake up electrified out of the coma by our
own souls' airplanes roaring over the roof they've come
to drop angelic bombs the hospital illuminates itself
imaginary walls collapse   O skinny legions run outside
O starry-spangled shock of mercy the eternal war is
here   O victory forget your underwear we're free
I'm with you in Rockland
in my dreams you walk dripping from a sea-journey on
the highway across America in tears to the door of my
cottage in the Western night

San Francisco 1955–56

Footnote to Howl

Holy! Holy! Holy! Holy! Holy! Holy! Holy! Holy! Holy! Holy!
　　Holy! Holy! Holy! Holy! Holy!
The world is holy! The soul is holy! The skin is holy! The nose
　　is holy! The tongue and cock and hand and asshole holy!
Everything is holy! everybody's holy! everywhere is holy!
　　everyday is in eternity! Everyman's an angel!
The bum's as holy as the seraphim! the madman is holy as you
　　my soul are holy!
The typewriter is holy the poem is holy the voice is holy the
　　hearers are holy the ecstasy is holy!
Holy Peter holy Allen holy Solomon holy Lucien holy Kerouac
　　holy Huncke holy Burroughs holy Cassady holy the
　　unknown buggered and suffering beggars holy the hideous
　　human angels!
Holy my mother in the insane asylum! Holy the cocks of the
　　grandfathers of Kansas!
Holy the groaning saxophone! Holy the bop apocalypse! Holy
　　the jazzbands marijuana hipsters peace peyote pipes &
　　drums!
Holy the solitudes of skyscrapers and pavements! Holy the
　　cafeterias filled with the millions! Holy the mysterious
　　rivers of tears under the streets!
Holy the lone juggernaut! Holy the vast lamb of the middle
　　class! Holy the crazy shepherds of rebellion! Who digs
　　Los Angeles IS Los Angeles!
Holy New York Holy San Francisco Holy Peoria & Seattle Holy
　　Paris Holy Tangiers Holy Moscow Holy Istanbul!

Holy time in eternity holy eternity in time holy the clocks
    in space holy the fourth dimension holy the fifth Inter-
    national holy the Angel in Moloch!

Holy the sea holy the desert holy the railroad holy the loco-
    motive holy the visions holy the hallucinations holy the
    miracles holy the eyeball holy the abyss!

Holy forgiveness! mercy! charity! faith! Holy! Ours! bodies!
    suffering! magnanimity!

Holy the supernatural extra brilliant intelligent kindness of the
    soul!

Berkeley, 1955

A Supermarket in California

What thoughts I have of you tonight, Walt Whitman, for I walked down the sidestreets under the trees with a headache self-conscious looking at the full moon.

In my hungry fatigue, and shopping for images, I went into the neon fruit supermarket, dreaming of your enumerations!

What peaches and what penumbras! Whole families shopping at night! Aisles full of husbands! Wives in the avocados, babies in the tomatoes!—and you, García Lorca, what were you doing down by the watermelons?

I saw you, Walt Whitman, childless, lonely old grubber, poking among the meats in the refrigerator and eyeing the grocery boys.

I heard you asking questions of each: Who killed the pork chops? What price bananas? Are you my Angel?

I wandered in and out of the brilliant stacks of cans following you, and followed in my imagination by the store detective.

We strode down the open corridors together in our solitary fancy tasting artichokes, possessing every frozen delicacy, and never passing the cashier.

Where are we going, Walt Whitman? The doors close in an hour. Which way does your beard point tonight?

(I touch your book and dream of our odyssey in the supermarket and feel absurd.)

Will we walk all night through solitary streets? The trees

add shade to shade, lights out in the houses, we'll both be lonely.

Will we stroll dreaming of the lost America of love past blue automobiles in driveways, home to our silent cottage?

Ah, dear father, graybeard, lonely old courage-teacher, what America did you have when Charon quit poling his ferry and you got out on a smoking bank and stood watching the boat disappear on the black waters of Lethe?

Berkeley, 1955

Transcription of Organ Music

The flower in the glass peanut bottle formerly in the kitchen
    crooked to take a place in the light,
the closet door opened, because I used it before, it kindly stayed
    open waiting for me, its owner.

I began to feel my misery in pallet on floor, listening to music,
    my misery, that's why I want to sing.
The room closed down on me, I expected the presence of the
    Creator, I saw my gray painted walls and ceiling, they
    contained my room, they contained me
as the sky contained my garden,
I opened my door

    The rambler vine climbed up the cottage post, the leaves
in the night still where the day had placed them, the animal
heads of the flowers where they had arisen
    to think at the sun

    Can I bring back the words? Will thought of transcrip-
tion haze my mental open eye?

    The kindly search for growth, the gracious desire to exist
of the flowers, my near ecstasy at existing among them
    The privilege to witness my existence—you too must
seek the sun . . .

My books piled up before me for my use

waiting in space where I placed them, they haven't disappeared, time's left its remnants and qualities for me to use—my words piled up, my texts, my manuscripts, my loves.

I had a moment of clarity, saw the feeling in the heart of things, walked out to the garden crying.

Saw the red blossoms in the night light, sun's gone, they had all grown, in a moment, and were waiting stopped in time for the day sun to come and give them . . .

Flowers which as in a dream at sunset I watered faithfully not knowing how much I loved them.

I am so lonely in my glory—except they too out there—I looked up—those red bush blossoms beckoning and peering in the window waiting in blind love, their leaves too have hope and are upturned top flat to the sky to receive—all creation open to receive—the flat earth itself.

The music descends, as does the tall bending stalk of the heavy blossom, because it has to, to stay alive, to continue to the last drop of joy.

The world knows the love that's in its breast as in the flower, the suffering lonely world.

The Father is merciful.

The light socket is crudely attached to the ceiling, after the house was built, to receive a plug which sticks in it alright, and serves my phonograph now . . .

The closet door is open for me, where I left it, since I left it open, it has graciously stayed open.

The kitchen has no door, the hole there will admit me should I wish to enter the kitchen.

I remember when I first got laid, H.P. graciously took my cherry, I sat on the docks of Provincetown, age 23, joyful, elevated in hope with the Father, the door to the womb was open to admit me if I wished to enter.

There are unused electricity plugs all over my house if I ever need them.

The kitchen window is open, to admit air . . .

The telephone—sad to relate—sits on the floor—I haven't the money to get it connected—

I want people to bow as they see me and say he is gifted with poetry, he has seen the presence of the Creator.

And the Creator gave me a shot of his presence to gratify my wish, so as not to cheat me of my yearning for him.

Berkeley, September 8, 1955

Sunflower Sutra

I walked on the banks of the tincan banana dock and sat down
    under the huge shade of a Southern Pacific locomotive
    to look at the sunset over the box house hills and cry.
Jack Kerouac sat beside me on a busted rusty iron pole, com-
    panion, we thought the same thoughts of the soul, bleak
    and blue and sad-eyed, surrounded by the gnarled steel
    roots of trees of machinery.
The oily water on the river mirrored the red sky, sun sank
    on top of final Frisco peaks, no fish in that stream, no
    hermit in those mounts, just ourselves rheumy-eyed and
    hungover like old bums on the riverbank, tired and wily.
Look at the Sunflower, he said, there was a dead gray shadow
    against the sky, big as a man, sitting dry on top of a pile
    of ancient sawdust—
—I rushed up enchanted—it was my first sunflower, memories
    of Blake—my visions—Harlem
and Hells of the Eastern rivers, bridges clanking Joes Greasy
    Sandwiches, dead baby carriages, black treadless tires
    forgotten and unretreaded, the poem of the riverbank,
    condoms & pots, steel knives, nothing stainless, only the
    dank muck and the razor-sharp artifacts passing into the
    past—
and the gray Sunflower poised against the sunset, crackly bleak
    and dusty with the smut and smog and smoke of olden
    locomotives in its eye—
corolla of bleary spikes pushed down and broken like a battered
    crown, seeds fallen out of its face, soon-to-be-toothless

mouth of sunny air, sunrays obliterated on its hairy head like a dried wire spiderweb,

leaves stuck out like arms out of the stem, gestures from the sawdust root, broke pieces of plaster fallen out of the black twigs, a dead fly in its ear,

Unholy battered old thing you were, my sunflower O my soul, I loved you then!

The grime was no man's grime but death and human locomotives,

all that dress of dust, that veil of darkened railroad skin, that smog of cheek, that eyelid of black mis'ry, that sooty hand or phallus or protuberance of artificial worse-than-dirt—industrial—modern—all that civilization spotting your crazy golden crown—

and those blear thoughts of death and dusty loveless eyes and ends and withered roots below, in the home-pile of sand and sawdust, rubber dollar bills, skin of machinery, the guts and innards of the weeping coughing car, the empty lonely tincans with their rusty tongues alack, what more could I name, the smoked ashes of some cock cigar, the cunts of wheelbarrows and the milky breasts of cars, wornout asses out of chairs & sphincters of dynamos—all these

entangled in your mummied roots—and you there standing before me in the sunset, all your glory in your form!

A perfect beauty of a sunflower! a perfect excellent lovely sunflower existence! a sweet natural eye to the new hip moon, woke up alive and excited grasping in the sunset shadow sunrise golden monthly breeze!

How many flies buzzed round you innocent of your grime, while you cursed the heavens of the railroad and your flower soul?

Poor dead flower? when did you forget you were a flower? when did you look at your skin and decide you were an impotent dirty old locomotive? the ghost of a locomotive? the specter and shade of a once powerful mad American locomotive?

You were never no locomotive, Sunflower, you were a sunflower!

And you Locomotive, you are a locomotive, forget me not!

So I grabbed up the skeleton thick sunflower and stuck it at my
    side like a scepter,

and deliver my sermon to my soul, and Jack's soul too, and
    anyone who'll listen,

—We're not our skin of grime, we're not our dread bleak
    dusty imageless locomotive, we're all beautiful golden
    sunflowers inside, we're blessed by our own seed &
    golden hairy naked accomplishment-bodies growing into
    mad black formal sunflowers in the sunset, spied on by
    our eyes under the shadow of the mad locomotive river-
    bank sunset Frisco hilly tincan evening sitdown vision.

Berkeley, 1955

America

America I've given you all and now I'm nothing.
America two dollars and twentyseven cents January 17, 1956.
I can't stand my own mind.
America when will we end the human war?
Go fuck yourself with your atom bomb.
I don't feel good don't bother me.
I won't write my poem till I'm in my right mind.
America when will you be angelic?
When will you take off your clothes?
When will you look at yourself through the grave?
When will you be worthy of your million Trotskyites?
America why are your libraries full of tears?
America when will you send your eggs to India?
I'm sick of your insane demands.
When can I go into the supermarket and buy what I need with
    my good looks?
America after all it is you and I who are perfect not the next
    world.
Your machinery is too much for me.
You made me want to be a saint.
There must be some other way to settle this argument.
Burroughs is in Tangiers I don't think he'll come back it's
    sinister.
Are you being sinister or is this some form of practical joke?
I'm trying to come to the point.
I refuse to give up my obsession.
America stop pushing I know what I'm doing.

America the plum blossoms are falling.
I haven't read the newspapers for months, everyday somebody
    goes on trial for murder.
America I feel sentimental about the Wobblies.
America I used to be a communist when I was a kid I'm not
    sorry.
I smoke marijuana every chance I get.
I sit in my house for days on end and stare at the roses in the
    closet.
When I go to Chinatown I get drunk and never get laid.
My mind is made up there's going to be trouble.
You should have seen me reading Marx.
My psychoanalyst thinks I'm perfectly right.
I won't say the Lord's Prayer.
I have mystical visions and cosmic vibrations.
America I still haven't told you what you did to Uncle Max after
    he came over from Russia.
I'm addressing you.
Are you going to let your emotional life be run by Time Maga-
    zine?
I'm obsessed by Time Magazine.
I read it every week.
Its cover stares at me every time I slink past the corner candy-
    store.
I read it in the basement of the Berkeley Public Library.
It's always telling me about responsibility. Businessmen are
    serious. Movie producers are serious. Everybody's ser-
    ious but me.
It occurs to me that I am America.
I am talking to myself again.

Asia is rising against me.
I haven't got a chinaman's chance.
I'd better consider my national resources.
My national resources consist of two joints of marijuana
    millions of genitals an unpublishable private literature

that goes 1400 miles an hour and twenty-five-thousand
mental institutions.
I say nothing about my prisons nor the millions of underprivi-
leged who live in my flowerpots under the light of five
hundred suns.
I have abolished the whorehouses of France, Tangiers is the
next to go.
My ambition is to be President despite the fact that I'm a
Catholic.

America how can I write a holy litany in your silly mood?
I will continue like Henry Ford my strophes are as individual as
his automobiles more so they're all different sexes.
America I will sell you strophes $2500 apiece $500 down on
your old strophe
America free Tom Mooney
America save the Spanish Loyalists
America Sacco & Vanzetti must not die
America I am the Scottsboro boys.
America when I was seven momma took me to Communist
Cell meetings they sold us garbanzos a handful per ticket
a ticket costs a nickel and the speeches were free every-
body was angelic and sentimental about the workers it
was all so sincere you have no idea what a good thing the
party was in 1835 Scott Nearing was a grand old man a real
mensch Mother Bloor the Silk-strikers' Ewig-Weibliche
made me cry I once saw the Yiddish orator Israel Amter
plain. Everybody must have been a spy.
America you don't really want to go to war.
America it's them bad Russians.
Them Russians them Russians and them Chinamen. And them
Russians.
The Russia wants to eat us alive. The Russia's power mad. She
wants to take our cars from out our garages.
Her wants to grab Chicago. Her needs a Red *Readers' Digest*.

Her wants our auto plants in Siberia. Him big bureau-
cracy running our fillingstations.
That no good. Ugh. Him make Indians learn read. Him need
big black niggers. Hah. Her make us all work sixteen
hours a day. Help.
America this is quite serious.
America this is the impression I get from looking in the televi-
sion set.
America is this correct?
I'd better get right down to the job.
It's true I don't want to join the Army or turn lathes in preci-
sion parts factories, I'm nearsighted and psychopathic
anyway.
America I'm putting my queer shoulder to the wheel.

Berkeley, January 17, 1956

In the Baggage Room at Greyhound

I

In the depths of the Greyhound Terminal
sitting dumbly on a baggage truck looking at the sky waiting
    for the Los Angeles Express to depart
worrying about eternity over the Post Office roof in the night-
    time red downtown heaven,
staring through my eyeglasses I realized shuddering these
    thoughts were not eternity, nor the poverty of our lives,
    irritable baggage clerks,
nor the millions of weeping relatives surrounding the buses
    waving goodbye,
nor other millions of the poor rushing around from city to city
    to see their loved ones,
nor an indian dead with fright talking to a huge cop by the
    Coke machine,
nor this trembling old lady with a cane taking the last trip of
    her life,
nor the red-capped cynical porter collecting his quarters and
    smiling over the smashed baggage,
nor me looking around at the horrible dream,
nor mustached negro Operating Clerk named Spade, dealing
    out with his marvelous long hand the fate of thousands
    of express packages,
nor fairy Sam in the basement limping from leaden trunk to
    trunk,
nor Joe at the counter with his nervous breakdown smiling
    cowardly at the customers,

26

nor the grayish-green whale's stomach interior loft where we
    keep the baggage in hideous racks,
hundreds of suitcases full of tragedy rocking back and forth
    waiting to be opened,
nor the baggage that's lost, nor damaged handles, nameplates
    vanished, busted wires & broken ropes, whole trunks
    exploding on the concrete floor,
nor seabags emptied into the night in the final warehouse.

II

Yet Spade reminded me of Angel, unloading a bus,
dressed in blue overalls black face official Angel's workman cap,
pushing with his belly a huge tin horse piled high with black
    baggage,
looking up as he passed the yellow light bulb of the loft
and holding high on his arm an iron shepherd's crook.

III

It was the racks, I realized, sitting myself on top of them now
    as is my wont at lunchtime to rest my tired foot,
it was the racks, great wooden shelves and stanchions posts and
    beams assembled floor to roof jumbled with baggage,
—the Japanese white metal postwar trunk gaudily flowered &
    headed for Fort Bragg,
one Mexican green paper package in purple rope adorned with
    names for Nogales,
hundreds of radiators all at once for Eureka,
crates of Hawaiian underwear,
rolls of posters scattered over the Peninsula, nuts to Sacra-
    mento,
one human eye for Napa,
an aluminum box of human blood for Stockton

and a little red package of teeth for Calistoga –
it was the racks and these on the racks I saw naked in electric
    light the night before I quit,
the racks were created to hang our possessions, to keep us
    together, a temporary shift in space,
God's only way of building the rickety structure of Time,
to hold the bags to send on the roads, to carry our luggage
    from place to place
looking for a bus to ride us back home to Eternity where the
    heart was left and farewell tears began.

IV

A swarm of baggage sitting by the counter as the transcontin-
    ental bus pulls in.
The clock registering 12:15 A.M., May 9, 1956, the second hand
    moving forward, red.
Getting ready to load my last bus.—Farewell, Walnut Creek
    Richmond Vallejo Portland Pacific Highway
Fleet-footed Quicksilver, God of transience.
One last package sits lone at midnight sticking up out of the
    Coast rack high as the dusty fluorescent light.

The wage they pay us is too low to live on. Tragedy reduced
    to numbers.
This for the poor shepherds. I am a communist.

Farewell ye Greyhound where I suffered so much, hurt my
    knee and scraped my hand and built my pectoral muscles
    big as vagina.

May 9, 1956

An Asphodel

O dear sweet rosy
           unattainable desire
. . . how sad, no way
           to change the mad
cultivated asphodel, the
           visible reality . . .

and skin's appalling
           petals—how inspired
to be so lying in the living
           room drunk naked
and dreaming, in the absence
           of electricity . . .
over and over eating the low root
           of the asphodel,
gray fate . . .

           rolling in generation
on the flowery couch
           as on a bank in Arden—
my only rose tonite's the treat
           of my own nudity.

Fall, 1953

Song

The weight of the world
      is love.
Under the burden
      of solitude,
under the burden
      of dissatisfaction

      the weight,
the weight we carry
      is love.

Who can deny?
      In dreams
it touches
      the body,
in thought
      constructs
a miracle,
      in imagination
anguishes
      till born
in human—

looks out of the heart
      burning with purity—
for the burden of life
      is love,

but we carry the weight
        wearily,
and so must rest
in the arms of love
        at last,
must rest in the arms
        of love.

No rest
        without love,
no sleep
        without dreams
of love—
        be mad or chill
obsessed with angels
        or machines,
the final wish
        is love
—cannot be bitter,
        cannot deny,
cannot withhold
        if denied:

the weight is too heavy

        —must give
for no return
        as thought
is given
        in solitude
in all the excellence
        of its excess.

The warm bodies
        shine together
in the darkness,

the hand moves
to the center
of the flesh,
the skin trembles
in happiness
and the soul comes
joyful to the eye—

yes, yes,
that's what
I wanted,
I always wanted,
I always wanted,
to return
to the body
where I was born.

San Jose, 1954

Wild Orphan

        Blandly mother
takes him strolling
            by railroad and by river
—he's the son of the absconded
            hot rod angel—
and he imagines cars
            and rides them in his dreams,

so lonely growing up among
            the imaginary automobiles
and dead souls of Tarrytown

        to create
out of his own imagination
            the beauty of his wild
forebears—a mythology
            he cannot inherit.

Will he later hallucinate
            his gods? Waking
among mysteries with
            an insane gleam
of recollection?

        The recognition—
something so rare
            in his soul,

met only in dreams
      —nostalgias
of another life.

A question of the soul.
      And the injured
losing their injury
      in their innocence
—a cock, a cross,
      an excellence of love.

And the father grieves
      in flophouse
complexities of memory
      a thousand miles
away, unknowing
      of the unexpected
youthful stranger
      bumming toward his door.

New York, April 13, 1952

In Back of the Real

railroad yard in San Jose
        I wandered desolate
in front of a tank factory
        and sat on a bench
near the switchman's shack.

A flower lay on the hay on
        the asphalt highway
—the dread hay flower
        I thought—It had a
brittle black stem and
        corolla of yellowish dirty
spikes like Jesus' inchlong
        crown, and a soiled
dry center cotton tuft
        like a used shaving brush
that's been lying under
        the garage for a year.

Yellow, yellow flower, and
        flower of industry,
tough spiky ugly flower,
        flower nonetheless,
with the form of the great yellow
        Rose in your brain!
This is the flower of the World.

San Jose, 1954

Kaddish

For
Naomi Ginsberg 1894–1956

I

Strange now to think of you, gone without corsets & eyes,
     while I walk on the sunny pavement of Greenwich
     Village.
downtown Manhattan, clear winter noon, and I've been up
     all night, talking, talking, reading the Kaddish aloud,
     listening to Ray Charles blues shout blind on the phono-
     graph
the rhythm the rhythm—and your memory in my head three
     years after—And read Adonais' last triumphant stanzas
     aloud—wept, realizing how we suffer—
And how Death is that remedy all singers dream of, sing,
     remember, prophesy as in the Hebrew Anthem, or the
     Buddhist Book of Answers—and my own imagination
     of a withered leaf—at dawn—
Dreaming back thru life, Your time—and mine accelerating
     toward Apocalypse,
the final moment—the flower burning in the Day—and what
     comes after,
looking back on the mind itself that saw an American city
a flash away, and the great dream of Me or China, or you
     and a phantom Russia, or a crumpled bed that never
     existed—

like a poem in the dark—escaped back to Oblivion—

No more to say, and nothing to weep for but the Beings in the
    Dream, trapped in its disappearance,

sighing, screaming with it, buying and selling pieces of phan-
    tom, worshipping each other,

worshipping the God included in it all—longing or inevit-
    ability?—while it lasts, a Vision—anything more?

It leaps about me, as I go out and walk the street, look back
    over my shoulder, Seventh Avenue, the battlements of
    window office buildings shouldering each other high,
    under a cloud, tall as the sky an instant—and the sky
    above—an old blue place.

or down the Avenue to the South, to—as I walk toward the
    Lower East Side—where you walked 50 years ago, little
    girl—from Russia, eating the first poisonous tomatoes of
    America—frightened on the dock—

then struggling in the crowds of Orchard Street toward what?—
    toward Newark—

toward candy store, first home-made sodas of the century, hand-
    churned ice cream in backroom on musty brownfloor
    boards—

Toward education marriage nervous breakdown, operation,
    teaching school, and learning to be mad, in a dream—
    what is this life?

Toward the Key in the window—and the great Key lays its head
    of light on top of Manhattan, and over the floor, and lays
    down on the sidewalk—in a single vast beam, moving, as
    I walk down First toward the Yiddish Theater—and the
    place of poverty

you knew, and I know, but without caring now—Strange to
    have moved thru Paterson, and the West, and Europe
    and here again,

with the cries of Spaniards now in the doorstoops doors and
    dark boys on the street, fire escapes old as you

—Tho you're not old now, that's left here with me—

Myself, anyhow, maybe as old as the universe—and I guess that

dies with us—enough to cancel all that comes—What
came is gone forever every time—

That's good! That leaves it open for no regret—no fear radia-
tors, lacklove, torture even toothache in the end—

Though while it comes it is a lion that eats the soul—and the
lamb, the soul, in us, alas, offering itself in sacrifice to
change's fierce hunger—hair and teeth—and the roar
of bonepain, skull bare, break rib, rot-skin, braintricked
Implacability.

Ai! ai! we do worse! We are in a fix! And you're out, Death let
you out, Death had the Mercy, you're done with your
century, done with God, done with the path thru it—
Done with yourself at last—Pure—Back to the Babe dark
before your Father, before us all—before the world—

There, rest. No more suffering for you. I know where you've
gone, it's good.

No more flowers in the summer fields of New York, no joy
now, no more fear of Louis,

and no more of his sweetness and glasses, his high school
decades, debts, loves, frightened telephone calls, concep-
tion beds, relatives, hands—

No more of sister Elanor,—she gone before you—we kept it
secret—you killed her—or she killed herself to bear with
you—an arthritic heart—But Death's killed you both—
No matter—

Nor your memory of your mother, 1915 tears in silent movies
weeks and weeks—forgetting, agrieve watching Marie
Dressler address humanity, Chaplin dance in youth,

or Boris Godounov, Chaliapin's at the Met, halling his voice of a
weeping Czar—by standing room with Elanor & Max—
watching also the Capitalists take seats in Orchestra,
white furs, diamonds,

with the YPSL's hitch-hiking thru Pennsylvania, in black
baggy gym skirts pants, photograph of 4 girls holding
each other round the waste, and laughing eye, too coy,
virginal solitude of 1920

all girls grown old, or dead, now, and that long hair in the
  grave—lucky to have husbands later—

You made it—I came too—Eugene my brother before (still
  grieving now and will gream on to his last stiff hand, as
  he goes thru his cancer—or kill—later perhaps—soon he
  will think—)

And it's the last moment I remember, which I see them all, thru
  myself, now—tho not you

I didn't foresee what you felt—what more hideous gape of bad
  mouth came first—to you—and were you prepared?

To go where? In that Dark—that—in that God? a radiance?
  A Lord in the Void? Like an eye in the black cloud in a
  dream? Adonoi at last, with you?

Beyond my remembrance! Incapable to guess! Not merely the
  yellow skull in the grave, or a box of worm dust, and a
  stained ribbon—Deathshead with Halo? can you believe
  it?

Is it only the sun that shines once for the mind, only the flash
  of existence, than none ever was?

Nothing beyond what we have—what you had—that so
  pitiful—yet Triumph,

to have been here, and changed, like a tree, broken, or flower—
  fed to the ground—but mad, with its petals, colored,
  thinking Great Universe, shaken, cut in the head, leaf
  stript, hid in an egg crate hospital, cloth wrapped, sore—
  freaked in the moon brain, Naughtless.

No flower like that flower, which knew itself in the garden, and
  fought the knife—lost

Cut down by an idiot Snowman's icy—even in the Spring—
  strange ghost thought—some Death—Sharp icicle in his
  hand—crowned with old roses—a dog for his eyes—cock
  of a sweatshop—heart of electric irons.

All the accumulations of life, that wear us out—clocks, bodies,
  consciousness, shoes, breasts—begotten sons—your
  Communism—'Paranoia' into hospitals.

You once kicked Elanor in the leg, she died of heart failure later. You of stroke. Asleep? within a year, the two of you, sisters in death. Is Elanor happy?

Max grieves alive in an office on Lower Broadway, lone large mustache over midnight Accountings, not sure. His life passes—as he sees—and what does he doubt now? Still dream of making money, or that might have made money, hired nurse, had children, found even your Immortality, Naomi?

I'll see him soon. Now I've got to cut through—to talk to you—as I didn't when you had a mouth.

Forever. And we're bound for that, Forever—like Emily Dickinson's horses—headed to the End.

They know the way—These Steeds—run faster than we think—it's our own life they cross—and take with them.

Magnificent, mourned no more, marred of heart, mind behind, married dreamed, mortal changed—Ass and face done with murder.

In the world, given, flower maddened, made no Utopia, shut under pine, almed in Earth, balmed in Lone, Jehovah, accept.

Nameless, One Faced, Forever beyond me, beginningless, endless, Father in death. Tho I am not there for this Prophecy, I am unmarried, I'm hymnless, I'm Heavenless, headless in blisshood I would still adore

Thee, Heaven, after Death, only One blessed in Nothingness, not light or darkness, Dayless Eternity—

Take this, this Psalm, from me, burst from my hand in a day, some of my Time, now given to Nothing—to praise Thee—But Death

This is the end, the redemption from Wilderness, way for the Wonderer, House sought for All, black handkerchief washed clean by weeping—page beyond Psalm—Last change of mine and Naomi—to God's perfect Darkness—Death, stay thy phantoms!

II

Over and over—refrain—of the Hospitals—still haven't written your history—leave it abstract—a few images

run thru the mind—like the saxaphone chorus of houses and years—remembrance of electrical shocks.

By long nites as a child in Paterson apartment, watching over your nervousness—you were fat—your next move—

By that afternoon I stayed home from school to take care of you—once and for all—when I vowed forever that once man disagreed with my opinion of the cosmos, I was lost—

By my later burden—vow to illuminate mankind—this is release of particulars—(mad as you)—(sanity a trick of agreement)—

But you stared out the window on the Broadway Church corner, and spied a mystical assassin from Newark,

So phoned the Doctor—'OK go way for a rest'—so I put on my coat and walked you downstreet—On the way a grammarschool boy screamed, unaccountably—'Where you goin Lady to Death'? I shuddered—

and you covered your nose with motheaten fur collar, gas mask against poison sneaked into downtown atmosphere, sprayed by Grandma—

And was the driver of the cheesebox Public Service bus a member of the gang? You shuddered at his face, I could hardly get you on—to New York, very Times Square, to grab another Greyhound—

where we hung around 2 hours fighting invisible bugs and jewish sickness—breeze poisoned by Roosevelt—

out to get you—and me tagging along, hoping it would end in a quiet room in a victorian house by a lake.

Ride 3 hours thru tunnels past all American industry, Bayonne preparing for World War II, tanks, gas fields, soda factories, diners, locomotive roundhouse fortress—into piney woods New Jersey Indians—calm towns—long roads thru sandy tree fields—

Bridges by deerless creeks, old wampum loading the streambed—down there a tomahawk or Pocahontas bone—and a million old ladies voting for Roosevelt in brown small houses, roads off the Madness highway—

perhaps a hawk in a tree, or a hermit looking for an owl-filled branch—

All the time arguing—afraid of strangers in the forward double seat, snoring regardless—what busride they snore on now?

'Allen, you don't understand—it's—ever since those 3 big sticks up my back—they did something to me in Hospital, they poisoned me, they want to see me dead—3 big sticks, 3 big sticks—

'The Bitch! Old Grandma! Last week I saw her, dressed in pants like an old man, with a sack on her back, climbing up the brick side of the apartment

'On the fire escape, with poison germs, to throw on me—at night—maybe Louis is helping her—he's under her power—

'I'm your mother, take me to Lakewood' (near where Graf Zeppelin had crashed before, all Hitler in Explosion) 'where I can hide.'

We got there—Dr Whatzis rest home—she hid behind a closet—demanded a blood transfusion.

We were kicked out—tramping with Valise to unknown shady lawn houses—dusk, pine trees after dark—long dead street filled with crickets and poison ivy—

I shut her up by now—big house REST HOME ROOMS—gave the landlady her money for the week—carried up the iron valise—sat on bed waiting to escape—

Neat room in attic with friendly bedcover—lace curtains—spinning wheel rug—Stained wallpaper old as Naomi. We were home.

I left on the next bus to New York—lay my head back in the last seat, depressed—the worst yet to come?—abandoning her, rode in torpor—I was only 12.

Would she hide in her room and come out cheerful for breakfast? Or lock her door and stare thru the window for side-street spies? Listen at keyholes for Hitlerian invisible gas? Dream in a chair—or mock me, by—in front of a mirror, alone?

12 riding the bus at nite thru New Jersey, have left Naomi to Parcae in Lakewood's haunted house—left to my own fate bus—sunk in a seat—all violins broken—my heart sore in my ribs—mind was empty—Would she were safe in her coffin—

Or back at Normal School in Newark, studying up on America in a black skirt—winter on the street without lunch—a penny a pickle—home at night to take care of Elanor in the bedroom—

First nervous breakdown was 1919—she stayed home from school and lay in a dark room for three weeks—something bad—never said what—every noise hurt—dreams of the creaks of Wall Street—

Before the grey Depression—went upstate New York—recovered—Lou took photo of her sitting crossleg on the grass—her long hair wound with flowers—smiling—playing lullabies on mandoline—poison ivy smoke in left-wing summer camps and me in infancy saw trees—

or back teaching school, laughing with idiots, the backward classes—her Russian specialty—morons with dreamy lips, great eyes, thin feet & sicky fingers, swaybacked, rachitic—

great heads pendulous over Alice in Wonderland, a blackboard full of C A T.

Naomi reading patiently, story out of a Communist fairy book—Tale of the Sudden Sweetness of The Dictator—Forgiveness of Warlocks—Armies Kissing—

Deathsheads Around the Green Table—The King & the Workers—Paterson Press printed them up in the 30's till she went mad, or they folded, both.

O Paterson! I got home late that nite. Louis was worried. How could I be so—didn't I think? I shouldn't have left her. Mad in Lakewood. Call the Doctor. Phone the home in the pines. Too late.

Went to bed exhausted, wanting to leave the world (probably that year newly in love with R—— my high school mind hero, jewish boy who came a doctor later—then silent neat kid—

I later laying down life for him, moved to Manhattan—followed him to college—Prayed on ferry to help mankind if admitted—vowed, the day I journeyed to Entrance Exam—

by being honest revolutionary labor lawyer—would train for that—inspired by Sacco Vanzetti, Norman Thomas, Debs, Altgeld, Sandburg, Poe—Little Blue Books. I wanted to be President, or Senator.

ignorant woe—later dreams of kneeling by R's shocked knees declaring my love of 1941—What sweetness he'd have shown me, tho, that I'd wished him & despaired—first love—a crush—

Later a mortal avalanche, whole mountains of homosexuality, Matterhorns of cock, Grand Canyons of asshole—weight on my melancholy head—

meanwhile I walked on Broadway imagining Infinity like a rubber ball without space beyond—what's outside?—coming home to Graham Avenue still melancholy passing the lone green hedges across the street, dreaming after the movies—)

The telephone rang at 2AM—Emergency—she'd gone mad—Naomi hiding under the bed screaming bugs of Mussolini—Help! Louis! Buba! Fascists! Death!—the landlady frightened—old fag attendant screaming back at her—

Terror, that woke the neighbors—old ladies on the second floor recovering from menopause—all those rags between thighs, clean sheets, sorry over lost babies—husbands ashen—children sneering at Yale, or putting oil in hair at CCNY—or trembling in Montclair State Teachers College like Eugene—

Her big leg crouched to her breast, hand outstretched Keep Away, wool dress on her thighs, fur coat dragged under the bed—she barricaded herself under bedspring with suitcases.

Louis in pyjamas listening to phone, frightened—do

now?—Who could know?—my fault, delivering her to soli-
tude?—sitting in the dark room on the sofa, trembling, to
figure out—

He took the morning train to Lakewood, Naomi
still under bed—thought he brought poison Cops—Naomi
screaming—Louis what happened to your heart then? Have
you been killed by Naomi's ecstasy?

Dragged her out, around the corner, a cab, forced her in
with valise, but the driver left them off at drugstore. Bus stop,
two hours' wait.

I lay in bed nervous in the 4-room apartment, the big bed
in living room, next to Louis' desk—shaking—he came home
that nite, late, told me what happened.

Naomi at the prescription counter defending herself
from the enemy—racks of children's books, douche bags, aspi-
rins, pots, blood—'Don't come near me—murderers! Keep
away! Promise not to kill me!'

Louis in horror at the soda fountain—with Lake-
wood girlscouts—coke addicts—nurses—busmen hung on
schedule—Police from country precinct, dumbed—and a priest
dreaming of pigs on an ancient cliff?

Smelling the air—Louis pointing to emptiness?—
Customers vomiting their cokes—or staring—Louis humili-
ated—Naomi triumphant—The Announcement of the Plot.
Bus arrives, the drivers won't have them on trip to New York.

Phonecalls to Dr Whatzis, 'She needs a rest,' The mental
hospital—State Greystone Doctors—'Bring her here, Mr Gins-
berg.'

Naomi, Naomi—sweating, bulge-eyed, fat, the dress
unbuttoned at one side—hair over brow, her stocking hanging
evilly on her legs—screaming for a blood transfusion—one
righteous hand upraised—a shoe in it—barefoot in the Phar-
macy—

The enemies approach—what poisons? Tape recorders?
FBI? Zhdanov hiding behind the counter? Trotsky mixing rat
bacteria in the back of the store? Uncle Sam in Newark, plot-

ting deathly perfumes in the Negro district? Uncle Ephraim, drunk with murder in the politician's bar, scheming of Hague? Aunt Rose passing water thru the needles of the Spanish Civil War?

till the hired $35 ambulance came from Red Bank—— Grabbed her arms—strapped her on the stretcher—moaning, poisoned by imaginaries, vomiting chemicals thru Jersey, begging mercy from Essex County to Morristown—

And back to Greystone where she lay three years—that was the last breakthrough, delivered her to Madhouse again—

On what wards—I walked there later, oft—old catatonic ladies, grey as cloud or ash or walls—sit crooning over floorspace—Chairs—and the wrinkled hags acreep, accusing—begging my 13-year-old mercy—

'Take me home'—I went alone sometimes looking for the lost Naomi, taking Shock—and I'd say, 'No, you're crazy Mama,—Trust the Drs.'—

And Eugene, my brother, her elder son, away studying Law in a furnished room in Newark—

came Paterson-ward next day—and he sat on the broken-down couch in the living room—'We had to send her back to Greystone'—

—his face perplexed, so young, then eyes with tears— then crept weeping all over his face—'What for?' wail vibrating in his cheekbones, eyes closed up, high voice—Eugene's face of pain.

Him faraway, escaped to an Elevator in the Newark Library, his bottle daily milk on windowsill of $5 week furn room downtown at trolley tracks—

He worked 8 hrs. a day for $20/wk—thru Law School years—stayed by himself innocent near negro whorehouses.

Unlaid, poor virgin—writing poems about Ideals and politics letters to the editor Pat Eve News—(we both wrote, denouncing Senator Borah and Isolationists—and felt mysterious toward Paterson City Hall—

I sneaked inside it once—local Moloch tower with phallus spire & cap o' ornament, strange gothic Poetry that stood on Market Street—replica Lyons' Hotel de Ville—

wings, balcony & scrollwork portals, gateway to the giant city clock, secret map room full of Hawthorne—dark Debs in the Board of Tax—Rembrandt smoking in the gloom—

Silent polished desks in the great committee room— Aldermen? Bd of Finance? Mosca the hairdresser aplot—Crapp the gangster issuing orders from the john—The madmen struggling over Zone, Fire, Cops & Backroom Metaphysics—we're all dead—outside by the bus-stop Eugene stared thru childhood—

where the Evangelist preached madly for 3 decades, hard-haired, cracked & true to his mean Bible—chalked Prepare to Meet Thy God on civic pave—

or God is Love on the railroad overpass concrete—he raved like I would rave, the lone Evangelist—Death on City Hall—)

But Gene, young,—been Montclair Teachers College 4 years—taught half year & quit to go ahead in life—afraid of Discipline Problems—dark sex Italian students, raw girls getting laid, no English, sonnets disregarded—and he did not know much—just that he lost—

so broke his life in two and paid for Law—read huge blue books and rode the ancient elevator 13 miles away in Newark & studied up hard for the future

just found the Scream of Naomi on his failure doorstep, for the final time, Naomi gone, us lonely—home—him sitting there—

Then have some chicken soup, Eugene. The Man of Evangel wails in front of City Hall. And this year Lou has poetic loves of suburb middle-age—in secret—music from his 1937 book—Sincere—he longs for beauty—

No love since Naomi screamed—since 1923?—now lost in Greystone ward—new shock for her—Electricity, following the 40 Insulin.

And Metrasol had made her fat.

So that a few years later she came home again—we'd much advanced and planned—I waited for that day—my Mother again to cook &—play the piano—sing at mandoline—Lung Stew, & Stenka Razin, & the communist line on the war with Finland—and Louis in debt—suspected to be poisoned money—mysterious capitalisms

—& walked down the long front hall & looked at the furniture. She never remembered it all. Some amnesia. Examined the doilies—and the dining room set was sold—

the Mahogany table—20 years love—gone to the junk man—we still had the piano—and the book of Poe—and the Mandolin, tho needed some string, dusty—

She went to the backroom to lay down in bed and ruminate, or nap, hide—I went in with her, not leave her by herself—lay in bed next to her—shades pulled, dusky, late afternoon—Louis in front room at desk, waiting—perhaps boiling chicken for supper—

'Don't be afraid of me because I'm just coming back home from the mental hospital—I'm your mother—'.

Poor love, lost—a fear—I lay there—Said, 'I love you Naomi,'—stiff, next to her arm. I would have cried, was this the comfortless lone union?—Nervous, and she got up soon.

Was she ever satisfied? And—by herself sat on the new couch by the front windows, uneasy—cheek leaning on her hand—narrowing eye—at what fate that day—

Picking her tooth with her nail, lips formed an O, suspicion—thought's old worn vagina—absent sideglance of eye—some evil debt written in the wall, unpaid—& the aged breasts of Newark come near—

May have heard radio gossip thru the wires in her head, controlled by 3 big sticks left in her back by gangsters in amnesia, thru the hospital—caused pain between her shoulders—

Into her head—Roosevelt should know her case, she told me—Afraid to kill her, now, that the government knew their names—traced back to Hitler—wanted to leave Louis' house forever.

One night, sudden attack—her noise in the bathroom—like croaking up her soul—convulsions and red vomit coming out of her mouth—diarrhea water exploding from her behind—on all fours in front of the toilet—urine running between her legs—left retching on the tile floor smeared with her black feces—unfainted—

At forty, varicosed, nude, fat, doomed, hiding outside the apartment door near the elevator calling Police, yelling for her girl-friend Rose to help—

Once locked herself in with razor or iodine—could hear her cough in tears at sink—Lou broke through glass green-painted door, we pulled her out to the bedroom.

Then quiet for months that winter—walks, alone, nearby on Broadway, read Daily Worker—Broke her arm, fell on icy street—

Began to scheme escape from cosmic financial murder plots—later she ran away to the Bronx to her sister Elanor. And there's another saga of late Naomi in New York.

Or thru Elanor or the Workman's Circle, where she worked, addressing envelopes, she made out—went shopping for Campbell's tomato soup—saved money Louis mailed her—

Later she found a boyfriend, and he was a doctor—Dr Isaac worked for National Maritime Union—now Italian bald and pudgy old doll—who was himself an orphan—but they kicked him out—Old cruelties—

Sloppier, sat around on bed or chair, in corset dreaming to herself—'I'm hot—I'm getting fat—I used to have such a beautiful figure before I went to the hospital—You should have seen me in Woodbine—' This in a furnished room around the NMU hall, 1943.

Looking at naked baby pictures in the magazine—baby powder advertisements, strained lamb carrots—'I will think nothing but beautiful thoughts.'

Revolving her head round and round on her neck at

window light in summertime, in hypnotize, in doven-dream recall—

'I touch his cheek, I touch his cheek, he touches my lips with his hand, I think beautiful thoughts, the baby has a beautiful hand.'—

Or a No-shake of her body, disgust—some thought of Buchenwald—some insulin passes thru her head—a grimace nerve shudder at Involuntary (as shudder when I piss)—bad chemical in her cortex—'No don't think of that. He's a rat.'

Naomi: 'And when we die we become an onion, a cabbage, a carrot, or a squash, a vegetable.' I come downtown from Columbia and agree. She reads the Bible, thinks beautiful thoughts all day.

'Yesterday I saw God. What did he look like? Well, in the afternoon I climbed up a ladder—he has a cheap cabin in the country, like Monroe, NY the chicken farms in the wood. He was a lonely old man with a white beard.

'I cooked supper for him. I made him a nice supper— lentil soup, vegetables, bread & butter—miltz—he sat down at the table and ate, he was sad.

'I told him, Look at all those fightings and killings down there, What's the matter? Why don't you put a stop to it?

'I try, he said—That's all he could do, he looked tired. He's a bachelor so long, and he likes lentil soup.'

Serving me meanwhile, a plate of cold fish—chopped raw cabbage dript with tapwater—smelly tomatoes—week-old health food—grated beets & carrots with leaky juice, warm—more and more disconsolate food—I can't eat it for nausea sometimes—the Charity of her hands stinking with Manhattan, madness, desire to please me, cold undercooked fish—pale red near the bones. Her smells—and oft naked in the room, so that I stare ahead, or turn a book ignoring her.

One time I thought she was trying to make me come lay her—flirting to herself at sink—lay back on huge bed that filled most of the room, dress up round her hips, big slash of hair, scars of operations, pancreas, belly wounds, abortions, appendix, stitching of incisions pulling down in the fat like hideous thick zippers—ragged long lips between her legs—What, even, smell of asshole? I was cold—later revolted a little, not much—seemed perhaps a good idea to try—know the Monster of the Beginning Womb—Perhaps—that way. Would she care? She needs a lover.

Yisborach, v'yistabach, v'yispoar, v'yisroman, v'yisnaseh, v'yishador, v'yishalleh, v'yishallol, sh'meh d'kudsho, b'rich hu.

And Louis reestablishing himself in Paterson grimy apartment in negro district—living in dark rooms—but found himself a girl he later married, falling in love again—tho sere & shy—hurt with 20 years Naomi's mad idealism.

Once I came home, after longtime in N.Y., he's lonely—sitting in the bedroom, he at desk chair turned round to face me—weeps, tears in red eyes under his glasses—

That we'd left him—Gene gone strangely into army—she out on her own in NY, almost childish in her furnished room. So Louis walked downtown to postoffice to get mail, taught in highschool—stayed at poetry desk, forlorn—ate grief at Bickford's all these years—are gone.

Eugene got out of the Army, came home changed and lone—cut off his nose in jewish operation—for years stopped girls on Broadway for cups of coffee to get laid—Went to NYU, serious there, to finish Law.—

And Gene lived with her, ate naked fishcakes, cheap, while she got crazier—He got thin, or felt helpless, Naomi striking 1920 poses at the moon, half-naked in the next bed.

bit his nails and studied—was the weird nurse-son—Next year he moved to a room near Columbia—though she wanted to live with her children—

'Listen to your mother's plea, I beg you'—Louis still sending her checks—I was in bughouse that year 8 months—my own visions unmentioned in this here Lament—

But then went half mad—Hitler in her room, she saw his mustache in the sink—afraid of Dr Isaac now, suspecting that he was in on the Newark plot—went up to Bronx to live near Elanor's Rheumatic Heart—

And Uncle Max never got up before noon, tho Naomi at 6 AM was listening to the radio for spies—or searching the windowsill,

for in the empty lot downstairs, an old man creeps with his bag stuffing packages of garbage in his hanging black overcoat.

Max's sister Edie works—17 years bookeeper at Gimbels— lived downstairs in apartment house, divorced—so Edie took in Naomi on Rochambeau Ave—

Woodlawn Cemetery across the street, vast dale of graves where Poe once—Last stop on Bronx subway—lots of communists in that area.

Who enrolled for painting classes at night in Bronx Adult High School—walked alone under Van Corlandt Elevated line to class—paints Naomiisms—

Humans sitting on the grass in some Camp No-Worry summers yore—saints with droopy faces and long-ill-fitting pants, from hospital—

Brides in front of Lower East Side with short grooms— lost El trains running over the Babylonian apartment rooftops in the Bronx—

Sad paintings—but she expressed herself. Her mandolin gone, all strings broke in her head, she tried. Toward Beauty? or some old life Message?

But started kicking Elanor, and Elanor had heart trouble— came upstairs and asked her about Spydom for hours,—Elanor frazzled. Max away at office, accounting for cigar stores till at night.

'I am a great woman—am truly a beautiful soul—and because of that they (Hitler, Grandma, Hearst, the Capitalists, Franco, Daily News, the 20's, Mussolini, the living dead) want to shut me up—Buba's the head of a spider network—'

Kicking the girls, Edie & Elanor—Woke Edie at midnite to tell her she was a spy and Elanor a rat. Edie worked all day and couldn't take it—She was organizing the union.—And Elanor began dying, upstairs in bed.

The relatives call me up, she's getting worse—I was the only one left—Went on the subway with Eugene to see her, ate stale fish—

'My sister whispers in the radio—Louis must be in the apartment—his mother tells him what to say—LIARS!—I cooked for my two children—I played the mandolin—'

Last night the nightingale woke me/ Last night when all was still/ it sang in the golden moonlight/ from on the wintry hill. She did.

I pushed her against the door and shouted 'DON'T KICK ELANOR!'—she stared at me—Contempt—die—disbelief her sons are so naive, so dumb—'Elanor is the worst spy! She's taking orders!'

'—No wires in the room!'—I'm yelling at her—last ditch, Eugene listening on the bed—what can he do to escape that fatal Mama—'You've been away from Louis years already—Grandma's too old to walk—'

We're all alive at once then—even me & Gene & Naomi in one mythological Cousinesque room—screaming at each other in the Forever—I in Columbia jacket, she half undressed.

I banging against her head which saw Radios, Sticks, Hitlers—the gamut of Hallucinations—for real—her own universe—no road that goes elsewhere—to my own—No America, not even a world—

That you go as all men, as Van Gogh, as mad Hannah, all the same—to the last doom—Thunder, Spirits, Lightning!

I've seen your grave! O strange Naomi! My own—cracked grave! Shema Y'Israel—I am Svul Avrum—you—in death?

Your last night in the darkness of the Bronx—I phone-called—thru hospital to secret police.

That came, when you and I were alone, shrieking at Elanor in my ear—who breathed hard in her own bed, got thin—

Nor will forget, the doorknock, at your fright of spies,—Law advancing, on my honor—Eternity entering the room—

you running to the bathroom undressed, hiding in protest from the last heroic fate—

    staring at my eyes, betrayed—the final cops of madness rescuing me—from your foot against the broken heart of Elanor,

    your voice at Edie weary of Gimbels coming home to broken radio—and Louis needing a poor divorce, he wants to get married soon—Eugene dreaming, hiding at 125 St., suing negroes for money on crud furniture, defending black girls—

    Protests from the bathroom—Said you were sane—dressing in a cotton robe, your shoes, then new, your purse and newspaper clippings—no—your honesty—

    as you vainly made your lips more real with lipstick, looking in the mirror to see if the Insanity was Me or a carful of police.

    or Grandma spying at 78—Your vision—Her climbing over the walls of the cemetery with political kidnapper's bag—or what you saw on the walls of the Bronx, in pink nightgown at midnight, staring out the window on the empty lot—

    Ah Rochambeau Ave—Playground of Phantoms—last apartment in the Bronx for spies—last home for Elanor or Naomi, here these communist sisters lost their revolution—

    'All right—put on your coat Mrs.—let's go—We have the wagon downstairs—you want to come with her to the station?'

    The ride then—held Naomi's hand, and held her head to my breast, I'm taller—kissed her and said I did it for the best—Elanor sick—and Max with heart condition—Needs—

    To me—'Why did you do this?'—'Yes Mrs., your son will have to leave you in an hour'—The Ambulance

    came in a few hours—drove off at 4 AM to some Bellevue in the night downtown—gone to the hospital forever. I saw her led away—she waved, tears in her eyes.

    Two years, after a trip to Mexico—bleak in the flat plain near Brentwood, scrub brush and grass around the unused RR train track to the crazyhouse—

new brick 20 story central building—lost on the vast lawns of madtown on Long Island—huge cities of the moon.

Asylum spreads out giant wings above the path to a minute black hole—the door—entrance thru crotch—

I went in—smelt funny—the halls again—up elevator—to a glass door on a Woman's Ward—to Naomi—Two nurses buxom white—They led her out, Naomi stared—and I gaspt—She'd had a stroke—

Too thin, shrunk on her bones—age come to Naomi—now broken into white hair—loose dress on her skeleton—face sunk, old! withered—cheek of crone—

One hand stiff—heaviness of forties & menopause reduced by one heart stroke, lame now—wrinkles—a scar on her head, the lobotomy—ruin, the hand dipping downwards to death—

O Russian faced, woman on the grass, your long black hair is crowned with flowers, the mandolin is on your knees—

Communist beauty, sit here married in the summer among daisies, promised happiness at hand—

holy mother, now you smile on your love, your world is born anew, children run naked in the field spotted with dandelions,

they eat in the plum tree grove at the end of the meadow and find a cabin where a white-haired negro teaches the mystery of his rainbarrel—

blessed daughter come to America, I long to hear your voice again, remembering your mother's music, in the Song of the Natural Front—

O glorious muse that bore me from the womb, gave suck first mystic life & taught me talk and music, from whose pained head I first took Vision—

Tortured and beaten in the skull—What mad hallucinations of the damned that drive me out of my own skull to seek Eternity till I find Peace for Thee, O Poetry—and for all humankind call on the Origin

Death which is the mother of the universe!—Now wear your nakedness forever, white flowers in your hair, your marriage sealed behind the sky—no revolution might destroy that maidenhood—

O beautiful Garbo of my Karma—all photographs from 1920 in Camp Nicht-Gedeiget here unchanged—with all the teachers from Newark—Nor Elanor be gone, nor Max await his specter—nor Louis retire from this High School—

Back! You! Naomi! Skull on you! Gaunt immortality and revolution come—small broken woman—the ashen indoor eyes of hospitals, ward greyness on skin—

'Are you a spy?' I sat at the sour table, eyes filling with tears—'Who are you? Did Louis send you?—The wires—'

in her hair, as she beat on her head—'I'm not a bad girl—don't murder me!—I hear the ceiling—I raised two children—'

Two years since I'd been there—I started to cry—She stared—nurse broke up the meeting a moment—I went into the bathroom to hide, against the toilet white walls

'The Horror' I weeping—to see her again—'The Horror'—as if she were dead thru funeral rot in—'The Horror!'

I came back she yelled more—they led her away—'You're not Allen—' I watched her face—but she passed by me, not looking—

Opened the door to the ward,—she went thru without a glance back, quiet suddenly—I stared out—she looked old—the verge of the grave—'All the Horror!'

Another year, I left NY—on West Coast in Berkeley cottage dreamed of her soul—that, thru life, in what form it stood in that body, ashen or manic, gone beyond joy—

near its death—with eyes—was my own love in its form, the Naomi, my mother on earth still—sent her long letter—& wrote hymns to the mad—Work of the merciful Lord of Poetry.

that causes the broken grass to be green, or the rock to break in grass—or the Sun to be constant to earth—Sun of all sunflowers and days on bright iron bridges—what shines on old hospitals—as on my yard—

Returning from San Francisco one night, Orlovsky in my room—Whalen in his peaceful chair—a telegram from Gene, Naomi dead—

Outside I bent my head to the ground under the bushes near the garage—knew she was better—

at last—not left to look on Earth alone—2 years of solitude—no one, at age nearing 60—old woman of skulls—once long-tressed Naomi of Bible—

or Ruth who wept in America—Rebecca aged in Newark—David remembering his Harp, now lawyer at Yale

or Svul Avrum—Israel Abraham—myself—to sing in the wilderness toward God—O Elohim!—so to the end—2 days after her death I got her letter—

Strange Prophecies anew! She wrote—'The key is in the window, the key is in the sunlight at the window—I have the key—Get married Allen don't take drugs—the key is in the bars, in the sunlight in the window.

Love,

your mother'

which is Naomi—

HYMMNN

In the world which He has created according to his will Blessed
    Praised
Magnified Lauded Exalted the Name of the Holy One Blessed
    is He!
In the house in Newark Blessed is He! In the madhouse Blessed
    is He! In the house of Death Blessed is He!
Blessed be He in homosexuality! Blessed be He in Paranoia!
    Blessed be He in the city! Blessed be He in the Book!

57

Blessed be He who dwells in the shadow! Blessed be He! Blessed be He!

Blessed be you Naomi in tears! Blessed be you Naomi in fears! Blessed Blessed Blessed in sickness!

Blessed be you Naomi in Hospitals! Blessed be you Naomi in solitude! Blest be your triumph! Blest be your bars! Blest be your last years' loneliness!

Blest be your failure! Blest be your stroke! Blest be the close of your eye! Blest be the gaunt of your cheek! Blest be your withered thighs!

Blessed be Thee Naomi in Death! Blessed be Death! Blessed be Death!

Blessed be He Who leads all sorrow to Heaven! Blessed be He in the end!

Blessed be He who builds Heaven in Darkness! Blessed Blessed Blessed be He! Blessed be He! Blessed be Death on us All!

III

Only to have not forgotten the beginning in which she drank cheap sodas in the morgues of Newark,

only to have seen her weeping on grey tables in long wards of her universe

only to have known the weird ideas of Hitler at the door, the wires in her head, the three big sticks

rammed down her back, the voices in the ceiling shrieking out her ugly early lays for 30 years,

only to have seen the time-jumps, memory lapse, the crash of wars, the roar and silence of a vast electric shock,

only to have seen her painting crude pictures of Elevateds running over the rooftops of the Bronx

her brothers dead in Riverside or Russia, her lone in Long Island writing a last letter—and her image in the sunlight

at the window
'The key is in the sunlight at the window in the bars the key is
    in the sunlight,'
only to have come to that dark night on iron bed by stroke
    when the sun gone down on Long Island
and the vast Atlantic roars outside the great call of Being to
    its own
to come back out of the Nightmare—divided creation—with
    her head lain on a pillow of the hospital to die
—in one last glimpse—all Earth one everlasting Light in the
    familiar blackout—no tears for this vision—
But that the key should be left behind—at the window—the
    key in the sunlight—to the living—that can take
that slice of light in hand—and turn the door—and look back
    see
Creation glistening backwards to the same grave, size of
    universe,
size of the tick of the hospital's clock on the archway over the
    white door—

IV

O mother
what have I left out
O mother
what have I forgotten
O mother
farewell
with a long black shoe
farewell
with Communist Party and a broken stocking
farewell
with six dark hairs on the wen of your breast
farewell
with your old dress and a long black beard around the vagina

farewell
with your sagging belly
with your fear of Hitler
with your mouth of bad short stories
with your fingers of rotten mandolines
with your arms of fat Paterson porches
with your belly of strikes and smokestacks
with your chin of Trotsky and the Spanish War
with your voice singing for the decaying overbroken workers
with your nose of bad lay with your nose of the smell of the
     pickles of Newark
with your eyes
with your eyes of Russia
with your eyes of no money
with your eyes of false China
with your eyes of Aunt Elanor in an oxygen tent
with your eyes of starving India
with your eyes pissing in the park
with your eyes of America taking a fall
with your eyes of your failure at the piano
with your eyes of your relatives in California
with your eyes of Ma Rainey dying in an ambulance
with your eyes of Czechoslovakia attacked by robots
with your eyes going to painting class at night in the Bronx
with your eyes of the killer Grandma you see on the horizon
     from the Fire-Escape
with your eyes running naked out of the apartment screaming
     into the hall
with your eyes being led away by policemen to an ambulance
with your eyes strapped down on the operating table
with your eyes with the pancreas removed
with your eyes of appendix operation
with your eyes of abortion
with your eyes of ovaries removed
with your eyes of shock
with your eyes of lobotomy

with your eyes of divorce
with your eyes of stroke
with your eyes alone
with your eyes
with your eyes
with your Death full of Flowers

V

Caw caw caw crows shriek in the white sun over grave stones
in Long Island
Lord Lord Lord Naomi underneath this grass my halflife and
my own as hers
caw caw my eye be buried in the same Ground where I stand
in Angel
Lord Lord great Eye that stares on All and moves in a black
cloud
caw caw strange cry of Beings flung up into sky over the
waving trees
Lord Lord O Grinder of giant Beyonds my voice in a boundless
field in Sheol
Caw caw the call of Time rent out of foot and wing an instant
in the universe
Lord Lord an echo in the sky the wind through ragged leaves
the roar of memory
caw caw all years my birth a dream caw caw New York the bus
the broken shoe the vast highschool caw caw all Visions
of the Lord
Lord Lord Lord caw caw caw Lord Lord Lord caw caw caw
Lord

Paris, December 1957 – New York 1959

```
          *
      *       *

   Poem
   Rocket
       .       .

       .       .

       .       .

       .       .

       .       .

     .           .

    . . . . . . . . .
    *****************
```

'*Be a Star-screwer!*'—Gregory Corso

Old moon my eyes are new moon with human footprint
no longer Romeo Sadface in drunken river Loony Pierre
  eyebrow, goof moon
O possible moon in Heaven we get to first of ageless constel-
  lations of names
as God is possible as All is possible so we'll reach another life.

Moon politicians earth weeping and warring in eternity
the not one star disturbed by screaming madmen from Holly-
  wood
oil tycoons from Romania making secret deals with flabby
  green Plutonians—
slave camps on Saturn Cuban revolutions on Mars?
Old life and new side by side, will Catholic church find Christ
  on Jupiter
Mohammed rave in Uranus will Buddha be acceptable on the
  stolid planets

or will we find Zoroastrian temples flowering on Neptune?

What monstrous new ecclesiastical design on the entire
    universe unfolds in the dying Pope's brain?

Scientist alone is true poet he gives us the moon

he promises the stars he'll make us a new universe if it comes
    to that

O Einstein I should have sent you my flaming mss.

O Einstein I should have pilgrimaged to your white hair!

O fellow travellers I write you a poem in Amsterdam in the
    Cosmos

where Spinoza ground his magic lenses long ago

I write you a poem long ago

already my feet are washed in death

Here I am naked without identity

with no more body than the fine black tracery of pen mark on
    soft paper

as star talks to star multiple beams of sunlight all the same
    myriad thought

in one fold of the universe where Whitman was

and Blake and Shelley saw Milton dwelling as in a starry
    temple

brooding in his blindness seeing all—

Now at last I can speak to you beloved brothers of an unknown
    moon

real Yous squatting in whatever form amidst Platonic Vapors
    of Eternity

I am another Star.

Will you eat my poems or read them

or gaze with aluminum blind plates on sunless pages?

do you dream or translate & accept data with indifferent droop-
    ings of antennae?

do I make sense to your flowery green receptor eyesockets? do
    you have visions of God?

Which way will the sunflower turn surrounded by millions of
    suns?

This is my rocket my personal rocket I send up my message
    Beyond
Someone to hear me there
My immortality
without steel or cobalt basalt or diamond gold or mercurial
    fire
without passports filing cabinets bits of paper warheads
without myself finally
pure thought
message all and everywhere the same
I send up my rocket to land on whatever planet awaits it
preferably religious sweet planets no money
fourth dimensional planets where Death shows movies
plants speak (courteously) of ancient physics and poetry itself
    is manufactured by the trees
the final Planet where the Great Brain of the Universe sits
    waiting for a poem to land in His golden pocket
joining the other notes mash-notes love-sighs complaints-
    musical shrieks of despair and the million unutterable
    thoughts of frogs
I send you my rocket of amazing chemical
more than my hair my sperm or the cells of my body
the speeding thought that flies upward with my desire as instan-
    taneous as the universe and faster than light
and leave all other questions unfinished for the moment to
    turn back to sleep in my dark bed on earth.

Amsterdam, October 4, 1957

Europe! Europe!

World world world
I sit in my room
imagine the future
sunlight falls on Paris
I am alone there is no
one whose love is perfect
man has been mad man's
love is not perfect I
have not wept enough
my breast will be heavy
till death the cities
are specters of cranks
of war the cities are
work & brick & iron &
smoke of the furnace of
selfhood makes tearless
eyes red in London but
no eye meets the sun

Flashed out of sky it
hits Lord Beaverbrook's
white modern solid
paper building leaned
in London's street to
bear last yellow beams
old ladies absently gaze
thru fog toward heaven

poor pots on windowsills
snake flowers to street
Trafalgar's fountains splash
on noon-warmed pigeons
Myself beaming in ecstatic
wilderness on St Paul's dome
seeing the light on London
or here on a bed in Paris
sunglow through the high
window on plaster walls

Meek crowd underground
saints perish creeps
streetwomen meet lacklove
under gaslamp and neon
no woman in house loves
husband in flower unity
nor boy loves boy soft
fire in breast politics
electricity scares downtown
radio screams for money
police light on TV screens
laughs at dim lamps in
empty rooms tanks crash
thru bombshell no dream
of man's joy is made movie
think factory pushes junk
autos tin dreams of Eros
mind eats its flesh in
geekish starvation and no
man's fuck is holy for
man's work is most war

Bony China hungers brain
wash over power dam and
America hides mad meat

in refrigerator Britain
cooks Jerusalem too long
France eats oil and dead
salad arms & legs in Africa
loudmouth devours Arabia
negro and white warring
against the golden nuptial
Russia manufacture feeds
millions but no drunk can
dream Mayakovsky's suicide
rainbow over machinery
and backtalk to the sun

I lie in bed in Europe
alone in old red under
wear symbolic of desire
for union with immortality
but man's love's not perfect
in February it rains
as once for Baudelaire
one hundred years ago
planes roar in the air
cars race thru streets
I know where they go
to death but that is OK
it is that death comes
before life that no man
has loved perfectly no one
gets bliss in time new
mankind is not born that
I weep for this antiquity
and herald the Millennium
for I saw the Atlantic sun
rayed down from a vast cloud
at Dover on the sea cliffs
tanker size of ant heaved

up on ocean under shining
cloud and seagull flying
thru sun light's endless
ladders streaming in Eternity
to ants in the myriad fields
of England to sun flowers
bent up to eat infinity's
minute gold dolphins leaping
thru Mediterranean rainbow
White smoke and steam in Andes
Asia's rivers glittering
blind poets deep in lone
Apollonic radiance on hillsides
littered with empty tombs

Paris, February 29, 1958

To Lindsay

Vachel, the stars are out
dusk has fallen on the Colorado road
a car crawls slowly across the plain
in the dim light the radio blares its jazz
the heartbroken salesman lights another cigarette
In another city 27 years ago
I see your shadow on the wall
you're sitting in your suspenders on the bed
the shadow hand lifts up a Lysol bottle to your head
your shade falls over on the floor

Paris, May 1958

Message

Since we had changed
rogered spun worked
wept and pissed together
I wake up in the morning
with a dream in my eyes
but you are gone in NY
remembering me Good
I love you I love you
& your brothers are crazy
I accept their drunk cases
It's too long that I have been alone
it's too long that I've sat up in bed
without anyone to touch on the knee, man
or woman I don't care what anymore, I
want love I was born for I want you with me now
Ocean liners boiling over the Atlantic
Delicate steelwork of unfinished skyscrapers
Back end of the dirigible roaring over Lakehurst
Six women dancing together on a red stage naked
The leaves are green on all the trees in Paris now
I will be home in two months and look you in the eyes

Paris, May 1958

To Aunt Rose

Aunt Rose—now—might I see you
with your thin face and buck tooth smile and pain
              of rheumatism—and a long black heavy shoe
                  for your bony left leg
      limping down the long hall in Newark on the running
carpet
                  past the black grand piano
                      in the day room
                          where the parties were
                  and I sang Spanish loyalist songs
                      in a high squeaky voice
                          (hysterical) the committee listening
                  while you limped around the room
                      collected the money—
      Aunt Honey, Uncle Sam, a stranger with a cloth arm
                  in his pocket
                      and huge young bald head
                          of Abraham Lincoln Brigade

—your long sad face
          your tears of sexual frustration
                  (what smothered sobs and bony hips
                      under the pillows of Osborne Terrace)
          —the time I stood on the toilet seat naked
              and you powdered my thighs with calamine
                  against the poison ivy—my tender
                      and shamed first black curled hairs

what were you thinking in secret heart then
knowing me a man already—
and I an ignorant girl of family silence on the thin pedestal
of my legs in the bathroom—Museum of Newark.
Aunt Rose
Hitler is dead, Hitler is in Eternity; Hitler is with
Tamburlane and Emily Brontë

Though I see you walking still, a ghost on Osborne Terrace
down the long dark hall to the front door
limping a little with a pinched smile
in what must have been a silken
flower dress
welcoming my father, the Poet, on his visit to Newark
—see you arriving in the living room
dancing on your crippled leg
and clapping hands his book
had been accepted by Liveright

Hitler is dead and Liveright's gone out of business
The Attic of the Past and *Everlasting Minute* are out of print
Uncle Harry sold his last silk stocking
Claire quit interpretive dancing school
Buba sits a wrinkled monument in Old
Ladies Home blinking at new babies

last time I saw you was the hospital
pale skull protruding under ashen skin
blue veined unconscious girl
in an oxygen tent
the war in Spain has ended long ago
Aunt Rose

Paris, June 1958

At Apollinaire's Grave

. . . voici le temps
Où l'on connaîtra l'avenir
Sans mourir de connaissance

I

I visited Père Lachaise to look for the remains of Apollinaire
the day the U.S. President appeared in France for the grand confer-
    ence of heads of state
so let it be the airport at blue Orly a springtime clarity in the air
    over Paris
Eisenhower winging in from his American graveyard
and over the froggy graves at Père Lachaise an illusory mist as
    thick as marijuana smoke
Peter Orlovsky and I walked softly thru Père Lachaise we both
    knew we would die
and so held temporary hands tenderly in a citylike miniature eter-
    nity
roads and streetsigns rocks and hills and names on everybody's
    house
looking for the lost address of a notable Frenchman of the Void
to pay our tender crime of homage to his helpless menhir
and lay my temporary American Howl on top of his silent Calli-
    gramme
for him to read between the lines with Xray eyes of Poet
as he by miracle had read his own death lyric in the Seine

73

I hope some wild kidmonk lay his pamphlet on my grave for
      God to read me on cold winter nights in heaven
already our hands have vanished from that place my hand
      writes now in a room in Paris Git-Le-Coeur
Ah William what grit in the brain you had what's death
I walked all over the cemetery and still couldn't find your grave
what did you mean by that fantastic cranial bandage in your
      poems
O solemn stinking deathshead what've you got to say nothing
      and that's barely an answer

You can't drive autos into a sixfoot grave tho the universe is
      mausoleum big enough for anything
the universe is a graveyard and I walk around alone in here
knowing that Apollinaire was on the same street 50 years
      ago
his madness is only around the corner and Genet is with us
      stealing books
the West is at war again and whose lucid suicide will set it all
      right
Guillaume Guillaume how I envy your fame your accomplish-
      ment for American letters
your Zone with its long crazy line of bullshit about death
come out of the grave and talk thru the door of my mind
issue new series of images oceanic haikus blue taxicabs in
      Moscow negro statues of Buddha
pray for me on the phonograph record of your former exist-
ence with a long sad voice and strophes of deep sweet music
      sad and scratchy as World War I
I've eaten the blue carrots you sent out of the grave and Van
      Gogh's ear and maniac peyote of Artaud
and will walk down the streets of New York in the black cloak
      of French poetry
improvising our conversation in Paris at Père Lachaise
and the future poem that takes its inspiration from the light
      bleeding into your grave

II

Here in Paris I am your guest O friendly shade
the absent hand of Max Jacob
Picasso in youth bearing me a tube of Mediterranean
myself attending Rousseau's old red banquet I ate his violin
great party at the Bateau Lavoir not mentioned in the text-
    books of Algeria
Tzara in the Bois de Boulogne explaining the alchemy of the
    machineguns of the cookoos
he weeps translating me into Swedish
well dressed in a violet tie and black pants
a sweet purple beard which emerged from his face like the
    moss hanging from the walls of Anarchism
he spoke endlessly of his quarrels with André Breton
whom he had helped one day trim his golden mustache
old Blaise Cendrars received me into his study and spoke
    wearily of the enormous length of Siberia
Jacques Vaché invited me to inspect his terrible collection of
    pistols
poor Cocteau saddened by the once marvellous Radiguet at his
    last thought I fainted
Rigaut with a letter of introduction to Death
and Gide praised the telephone and other remarkable inventions
we agreed in principle though he gossiped of lavender underwear
but for all that he drank deeply of the grass of Whitman and
    was intrigued by all lovers named Colorado
princes of America arriving with their armfuls of shrapnel and
    baseball
Oh Guillaume the world so easy to fight seemed so easy
did you know the great political classicists would invade
    Montparnasse
with not one sprig of prophetic laurel to green their foreheads
not one pulse of green in their pillows no leaf left from their
    wars—Mayakovsky arrived and revolted

III

Came back sat on a tomb and stared at your rough menhir
a piece of thin granite like an unfinished phallus
a cross fading into the rock 2 poems on the stone one Coeur
     Renversée
other Habituez-vous comme moi A ces prodiges que j'annonce
     Guillaume Apollinaire de Kostrowitsky
someone placed a jam bottle filled with daisies and a 5&10¢
     surrealist typist ceramic rose
happy little tomb with flowers and overturned heart
under a fine mossy tree beneath which I sat snaky trunk
summer boughs and leaves umbrella over the menhir and
     nobody there
Et quelle voix sinistre ulule Guillaume qu'es-tu devenu
his nextdoor neighbor is a tree
there underneath the crossed bones heaped and yellow cranium
     perhaps
and the printed poems Alcools in my pocket his voice in the
     museum
Now middleage footsteps walk the gravel
a man stares at the name and moves toward the crematory
     building
same sky rolls over thru clouds as Mediterranean days on the
     Riviera during war
drinking Apollo in love eating occasional opium he'd taken the
     light
One must have felt the shock in St. Germain when he went out
     Jacob & Picasso coughing in the dark
a bandage unrolled and the skull left still on a bed outstretched
     pudgy fingers the mystery and ego gone
a bell tolls in the steeple down the street birds warble in the
     chestnut trees
Famille Bremont sleeps nearby Christ hangs big chested and
     sexy in their tomb

my cigarette smokes in my lap and fills the page with smoke
    and flames
an ant runs over my corduroy sleeve the tree I lean on grows
    slowly
bushes and branches upstarting through the tombs one silky
    spiderweb gleaming on granite
I am buried here and sit by my grave beneath a tree

Paris, Winter – Spring 1958

The Lion for Real

'Soyez muette pour moi, Idole contemplative . . .'

I came home and found a lion in my living room
Rushed out on the fire-escape screaming Lion! Lion!
Two stenographers pulled their brunette hair and banged the
     window shut
I hurried home to Paterson and stayed two days.

Called up my old Reichian analyst
who'd kicked me out of therapy for smoking marijuana
'It's happened' I panted 'There's a Lion in my room'
'I'm afraid any discussion would have no value' he hung up.

I went to my old boyfriend we got drunk with his girlfriend
I kissed him and announced I had a lion with a mad gleam in
     my eye
We wound up fighting on the floor I bit his eyebrow & he
     kicked me out
I ended masturbating in his jeep parked in the street moaning
     'Lion.'

Found Joey my novelist friend and roared at him 'Lion!'
He looked at me interested and read me his spontaneous ignu
     high poetries
I listened for lions all I heard was Elephant Tiglon Hippogryph
     Unicorn Ants
But figured he really understood me when we made it in Ignaz
     Wisdom's bathroom.

But next day he sent me a leaf from his Smokey Mountain
    retreat
'I love you little Bo-Bo with your delicate golden lions
But there being no Self and No Bars therefore the Zoo of your
    dear Father hath no Lion
You said your mother was mad don't expect me to produce the
    Monster for your Bridegroom.'

Confused dazed and exalted bethought me of real lion starved
    in his stink in Harlem
Opened the door the room was filled with the bomb blast of
    his anger
He roaring hungrily at the plaster walls but nobody could hear
    him outside thru the window
My eye caught the edge of the red neighbor apartment building
    standing in deafening stillness

We gazed at each other his implacable yellow eye in the red
    halo of fur
Waxed rheumy on my own but he stopped roaring and bared
    a fang greeting.
I turned my back and cooked broccoli for supper on an iron
    gas stove
boilt water and took a hot bath in the old tub under the sink
    board.

He didn't eat me, tho I regretted him starving in my presence.
Next week he wasted away a sick rug full of bones wheaten
    hair falling out
enraged and reddening eye as he lay aching huge hairy head
    on his paws
by the egg-crate bookcase filled up with thin volumes of Plato,
    & Buddha.

Sat by his side every night averting my eyes from his hungry
    motheaten face

stopped eating myself he got weaker and roared at night while
    I had nightmares
Eaten by lion in bookstore on Cosmic Campus, a lion myself
    starved by Professor Kandisky, dying in a lion's flophouse
    circus,
I woke up mornings the lion still added dying on the floor—
    'Terrible Presence!' I cried 'Eat me or die!'

It got up that afternoon—walked to the door with its paw on
    the wall to steady its trembling body
Let out a soul rending creak from the bottomless roof of his
    mouth
thundering from my floor to heaven heavier than a volcano at
    night in Mexico
Pushed the door open and said in a gravelly voice 'Not this
    time Baby—but I will be back again.'

Lion that eats my mind now for a decade knowing only your
    hunger
Not the bliss of your satisfaction O roar of the Universe how
    am I chosen
In this life I have heard your promise I am ready to die I have
    served
Your starved and ancient Presence O Lord I wait in my room
    at your Mercy.

Paris, March 1958

Ignu

On top of that if you know me I pronounce you an ignu
Ignu knows nothing of the world
a great ignoramus in factories though he may own or inspire
     them or even be production manager
Ignu has knowledge of the angel indeed ignu is angel in comical
     form
W. C. Fields Harpo Marx ignus Whitman an ignu
Rimbaud a natural ignu in his boy pants
The ignu may be queer though like not kind ignu blows arch-
     angels for the strange thrill
a gnostic women love him Christ overflowed with trembling
     semen for many a dead aunt
He's a great cocksman most beautiful girls are worshipped by
     ignu
Hollywood dolls or lone Marys of Idaho long-legged publicity
     women and secret housewives
have known ignu in another lifetime and remember their lover
Husbands also are secretly tender to ignu their buddy
oldtime friendship can do anything cuckold bugger drunk
     trembling and happy
Ignu lives only once and eternally and knows it
he sleeps in everybody's bed everyone's lonesome for ignu ignu
     knew solitude early
So ignu's a primitive of cock and mind
equally the ignu has written liverish tomes personal meta-
     physics abstract
images that scratch the moon 'lightningflash-flintspark' naked
     lunch fried shoes adios king

The shadow of the angel is waving in the opposite direction

dawn of intelligence turns the telephones into strange animals

he attacks the rose garden with his mystical shears snip snip
    snip

Ignu has painted Park Avenue with his own long melancholy

and ignu giggles in a hard chair over tea in Paris bald in his
    decaying room a black hotel

Ignu with his wild mop walks by Colosseum weeping

he plucks a clover from Keats' grave & Shelley's a blade of
    grass

knew Coleridge they had slow hung-up talks at midnight over
    tables of mahogany in London

sidestreet rooms in wintertime rain outside fog the cabman
    blows his hand

Charles Dickens is born ignu hears the wail of the babe

Ignu goofs nights under bridges and laughs at battleships

ignu is a battleship without guns in the North Sea lost O the
    flowerness of the moment

he knows geography he was there before he'll get out and die
    already

reborn a bearded humming Jew of Arabian mournful jokes

man with a star on his forehead and halo over his cranium

listening to music musing happy at the fall of a leaf the moon-
    light of immortality in his hair

table-hopping most elegant comrade of all most delicate
    mannered in the Sufi court

he wasn't even there at all

wearing zodiacal blue sleeves and the long peaked conehat of
    a magician

harkening to the silence of a well at midnight under a red star

in the lobby of Rockefeller Center attentive courteous bare-
    eyed enthusiastic with or without pants

he listens to jazz as if he were a negro afflicted with jewish
    melancholy and white divinity

Ignu's a natural you can see it when he pays the cabfare
    abstracted

pulling off the money from an impossible saintly roll
or counting his disappearing pennies to give to the strange bus-
     driver whom he admires
Ignu has sought you out he's the seeker of God
and God breaks down the world for him every ten years
he sees lightning flash in empty daylight when the sky is blue
he hears Blake's disembodied Voice recite the Sunflower in a
     room in Harlem
No woe on him surrounded by 700 thousand mad scholars
     moths fly out of his sleeve
He wants to die give up go mad break through into Eternity
live on and teach an aged saint or break down to an eyebrow
     clown
All ignus know each other in a moment's talk and measure
     each other up at once
as lifetime friends romantic winks and giggles across conti-
     nents
sad moment paying the cab goodby and speeding away uptown
One or two grim ignus in the pack
one laughing monk in dungarees
one delighted by cracking his eggs in an egg cup
one chews gum to music all night long rock and roll
one anthropologist cookoo in the Petén Rainforest
one sits in jail all year and bets karmaic racetrack
one chases girls down East Broadway into the horror movie
one pulls out withered grapes and rotten onions from his
     pants
one has a nannygoat under his bed to amuse visitors plasters
     the wall with his crap
collects scorpions whiskies skies etc. would steal the moon if
     he could find it
That would set fire to America but none of these make ignu
it's the soul that makes the style the tender firecracker of his
     thought
the amity of letters from strange cities to old friends
and the new radiance of morning on a foreign bed

A comedy of personal being his grubby divinity
Eliot probably an ignu one of the few who's funny when he eats
Williams of Paterson a dying American ignu
Burroughs a purest ignu his haircut is a cream his left finger
      pinkey chopped off for early ignu reasons metaphysical spells
         love spells with psychoanalysts
his very junkhood an accomplishment beyond a million dollars
Céline himself an old ignu over prose
I saw him in Paris dirty old gentleman of ratty talk
with longhaired cough three wormy sweaters round his neck
brown mould under historic fingernails
pure genius his giving morphine all night to 1400 passengers on
         a sinking ship
'because they were all getting emotional'
Who's amazing you is ignu communicate with me
by mail post telegraph phone street accusation or scratching
         at my window
and send me a true sign I'll reply special delivery
DEATH IS A LETTER THAT WAS NEVER SENT
Knowledge born of stamps words coins pricks jails seasons
         sweet ambition laughing gas
history with a gold halo photographs of the sea painting a
         celestial din in the bright window
one eye in a black cloud
and the lone vulture on a sand plain seen from the window of
         a Turkish bus
It must be a trick.   Two diamonds in the hand one Poetry one
         Charity
proves we have dreamed   and the long sword of intelligence
over which I constantly stumble like my pants at the age six—
         embarrassed.

New York, November, 1958

Death to Van Gogh's Ear!

POET is Priest
Money has reckoned the soul of America
Congress broken thru to the precipice of Eternity
the President built a War machine which will vomit and rear up
     Russia out of Kansas
The American Century betrayed by a mad Senate which no
     longer sleeps with its wife
Franco has murdered Lorca the fairy son of Whitman
just as Mayakovsky committed suicide to avoid Russia
Hart Crane distinguished Platonist committed suicide to cave
     in the wrong America
just as millions of tons of human wheat were burned in secret
     caverns under the White House
while India starved and screamed and ate mad dogs full of rain
and mountains of eggs were reduced to white powder in the
     halls of Congress
no godfearing man will walk there again because of the stink
     of the rotten eggs of America
and the Indians of Chiapas continue to gnaw their vitaminless
     tortillas
aborigines of Australia perhaps gibber in the eggless wilder-
     ness
and I rarely have an egg for breakfast tho my work requires
     infinite eggs to come to birth in Eternity
eggs should be eaten or given to their mothers
and the grief of the countless chickens of America is expressed
     in the screaming of her comedians over the radio

Detroit has built a million automobiles of rubber trees and
      phantoms
but I walk, I walk, and the Orient walks with me, and all Africa
      walks
and sooner or later North America will walk
for as we have driven the Chinese Angel from our door he will
      drive us from the Golden Door of the future
we have not cherished pity on Tanganyika
Einstein alive was mocked for his heavenly politics
Bertrand Russell driven from New York for getting laid
immortal Chaplin driven from our shores with the rose in his
      teeth
a secret conspiracy by Catholic Church in the lavatories of
      Congress has denied contraceptives to the unceasing
      masses of India.
Nobody publishes a word that is not the cowardly robot ravings
      of a depraved mentality
the day of the publication of the true literature of the Ameri-
      can body will be day of Revolution
the revolution of the sexy lamb
the only bloodless revolution that gives away corn
poor Genet will illuminate the harvesters of Ohio
Marijuana is a benevolent narcotic but J. Edgar Hoover prefers
      his deathly scotch
And the heroin of Lao-Tze & the Sixth Patriarch is punished by
      the electric chair
but the poor sick junkies have nowhere to lay their heads
fiends in our government have invented a cold-turkey cure
      for addiction as obsolete as the Defense Early Warning
      Radar System.
I am the defense early warning radar system
I see nothing but bombs
I am not interested in preventing Asia from being Asia
and the governments of Russia and Asia will rise and fall but
      Asia and Russia will not fall

the government of America also will fall but how can America
    fall
I doubt if anyone will ever fall anymore except governments
fortunately all the governments will fall
the only ones which won't fall are the good ones
and the good ones don't yet exist
But they have to begin existing they exist in my poems
they exist in the death of the Russian and American governments
they exist in the death of Hart Crane & Mayakovsky
Now is the time for prophecy without death as a consequence
the universe will ultimately disappear
Hollywood will rot on the windmills of Eternity
Hollywood whose movies stick in the throat of God
Yes Hollywood will get what it deserves
Time
Seepage of nerve-gas over the radio
History will make this poem prophetic and its awful silliness a
    hideous spiritual music
I have the moan of doves and the feather of ecstasy
Man cannot long endure the hunger of the cannibal abstract
War is abstract
the world will be destroyed
but I will die only for poetry, that will save the world
Monument to Sacco & Vanzetti not yet financed to ennoble
    Boston
natives of Kenya tormented by idiot con-men from England
South Africa in the grip of the white fool
Vachel Lindsay Secretary of the Interior
Poe Secretary of Imagination
Pound Secty. Economics
and Kra belongs to Kra, and Pukti to Pukti
crossfertilization of Blok and Artaud
Van Gogh's Ear on the currency
no more propaganda for monsters
and poets should stay out of politics or become monsters

I have become monsterous with politics

the Russian poet undoubtedly monsterous in his secret note-
book

Tibet should be left alone

These are obvious prophecies

America will be destroyed

Russian poets will struggle with Russia

Whitman warned against this 'fabled Damned of nations'

Where was Theodore Roosevelt when he sent out ultimatums
from his castle in Camden

Where was the House of Representatives when Crane read
aloud from his prophetic books

What was Wall Street scheming when Lindsay announced the
doom of Money

Were they listening to my ravings in the locker rooms of Bick-
fords Employment Offices?

Did they bend their ears to the moans of my soul when I strug-
gled with market research statistics in the Forum at Rome?

No they were fighting in fiery offices, on carpets of heartfailure,
screaming and bargaining with Destiny

fighting the Skeleton with sabres, muskets, buck teeth, indiges-
tion, bombs of larceny, whoredom, rockets, pederasty,

back to the wall to build up their wives and apartments, lawns,
suburbs, fairydoms,

Puerto Ricans crowded for massacre on 114th St. for the sake of
an imitation Chinese-Moderne refrigerator

Elephants of mercy murdered for the sake of an Elizabethan
birdcage

millions of agitated fanatics in the bughouse for the sake of the
screaming soprano of industry

Money-chant of soapers—toothpaste apes in television sets—
deodorizers on hypnotic chairs—

petroleum mongers in Texas—jet plane streaks among the
clouds—

sky writers liars in the face of Divinity—fanged butchers of

hats and shoes, all Owners! Owners! Owners! with obses-
sion on property and vanishing Selfhood!
and their long editorials on the fence of the screaming negro
attacked by ants crawled out of the front page!
Machinery of a mass electrical dream! A war-creating Whore
of Babylon bellowing over Capitols and Academies!
Money! Money! Money! shrieking mad celestial money of illu-
sion! Money made of nothing, starvation, suicide! Money
of failure! Money of death!
Money against Eternity! and eternity's strong mills grind out
vast paper of Illusion!

Paris, December 1957

Laughing Gas

To Gary Snyder
The red tin begging cup you gave me,
I lost it but its contents are undisturbed.

I

High on Laughing Gas
I've been here before
the odd vibration of
the same old universe

the nasal whine of the dentist's drill
    singing against the nostalgic
        piano Muzak in the wall
insistent, familiar, penetrating
    the teeth, where've I heard that
        asshole jazz before?

The universe is a void
   in which there is a dreamhole
The dream disappears
      the hold closes

It's the instant of going
into or coming out of
existence that is

important—to catch on
to the secret of the magic
        box

Stepping outside the universe
        by means of Nitrous Oxide
anesthetizing mind-consciousness

        the chiliasm was an impersonal dream—
one of many, being mere dreams.

        the sadness of birth
        and death, the sadness of
changing from dream to dream,
   the constant farewell
   of forms . . .
                saying ungoodby to what
didn't exist

The many worlds that don't exist
all which seem real
all joke
all lost cartoon

At that moment the whole goofy-spooky of the Universe WHAT?!
Joke Being slips into Nothing like the tail of a lizard disappearing
into a crack in the Wall with the final receding eyehole ending
Loony Tunes accompanied by Woody Woodpecker's hindoo maniac
laughter in the skull. Nobody gets hurt. They all disappear. They
were never there. Beginningless perfection.

        That's why Satori's accompanied by laughter
        and the Zenmaster rips up the Sutras in fury.

And the pain of this contrariety
The cycles of scream and laughter
faces and asses Christs and Buddhas
each with his own universe dragged
over the snowy mental poles
like a sack mad Santa Clauses
Worst pain in the dentist's chair comes true
novacain also arrives in the cycle
every hap will have its chance
even God will come Once or Twice
Satan will be my personal enemy

Relax and die—
The process will repeat itself
Be Born! Be Born!
Back to the same old smiling
                    dentist—

The Bloomfield police car
        with its idiot red light
        revolving on its head
        balefully at Eternity
                gone in an instant
                —simultaneous
                appearance of Bankrobbers
        at the Twentieth Century Bank
The fire engines screaming
        toward an old lady's
        burned-in-her-bedroom
        today apocalypse
            tomorrow
        Mickey Mouse cartoons—

I'm disgusted! it's Unbelievable!
What a funny horrible
        dirty joke!

The whole universe a shaggy dog story!
    with a weird ending that begins again
      till you get the point
'It was a dark and gloomy night . . .'
      'in every direction in and
        out'
         'You take the high road
    and I'll take the low'
              —everybody lost
in Scotlands of mind-consciousness—

      Adonoi Echad!
It is not One, but Two,
    not two but Infinite—
the universe be born and die
    in endless series in the mind!

Gary Snyder, Jack, Zen thinkers
    split open existence
    and laugh & Cry—
what's shock? what's measure?
    when the Mind's an irrational
      traffic light in
        Gobi—
follow the blinking lights of contrariety!

What's the use avoiding rats
and horror, hiding from Cops
    and dentists' drills?
Somebody will invent
    a Buchenwald next door
– an ant's dream's
    funnier than
      ours
– he has more of them

faster and seems
to give less of
a shit—

O waves of probable
and improbable
Universes—
Everybody's right

I'll finish this poem
in my next life.

II

. . . . with eye opening
slowly to perceive
that I be coming out
of a trance—
one look at the lipstick
it's a nurse
in a dentist's office

that first frog
thought leaping out of
the void

. . . a glimpse
out of which the whole
process unfolds this
universe & logically
and symmetrically next
unbuilds it in exact
reverse till you arrive
back at the Nothing
in which one chance

note was originally
struck . . .

      , the Czardas
of Creation, the first banal chord
establishing Music forever in
    its mechanical jukebox
      . . . and the whole
    structive unfolds
itself inevitably and
    folds back into
Nothing again . . .

—the same man
crossing the street looking
both ways watch out for
the cars—

and each time, returning
with a jerk of the face
('praps a dental touch)
dictated by the sinking
sensation, Oof! I've
been hoodwinked—

     again like
    someone in the Circus
defying death, got thrown
    into the orchestra—
      Note the music blaring
with an indifferent flourish of Triumph
     a nightmare Razz
    —as the acrobat leaps
out into the void—

Me! I made that Last Chance
     jump off the wire
way high up in the Big Top
          long ago . . .
                    it's happening again!
     I wake up dazed . . .

     it being the dream
of someone in a dentist's
chair in a Universe he
imagines—coming out
of gas—
     it's only happening
in the closed universe of
     illusion

III

A nice day in the Universe on Broad Street—sun shines today as it never shone before and never will again—stillness in the blue sky—the church's gold dome across the park sending and receiving flashes of light—I feel heart sick to destroy this all—

What hope have the children in their prams passing the white silent doors of the houses—only the Public Library knows.

Premonition in the dentist's chair—mechanical voices over the radio singing Destination Moon—mysterious sorrow for the moon of this forgotten universe—humans, singing, singing—of the moon—for money?—except it's the imbecilic canned voice of eternity rocking & rolling in Space making invisible announcements—

The Doc's agreed to the experiment—novacain, my mouth's begun to disappear first—like the Cheshire Cat.

BACK: Endless cycles of conflict happening in nothingness
make it impossible to grasp for the perfection
which does not exist
but is not necessary
so everything is final and occurs over & over again
till we will finally blank out as expected.

The First Note of Creation:
the only one there could be if there
weren't nothing but
an idea that there might
not be nothing—

Sherman Adams will resign
I'm holding my breath
the shiver run thru my belly
the nurse will be singing I love you
between breaths the Buddhists are right
a tear
siffle in the cheek
the possibility escape
the eye glare thru glasses
Nothing grasped at & ungrasped as its trance thought passes

I take my pen in hand
The same old way sings Sinatra
I'm writing to You give me understanding
I pray sings Sinatra
Can I never glimpse the round we have made?
Write me as soon as able sings Sinatra
O Lord burn me out of existence.

You've got a long body sings Sinatra
I refuse to breathe and return to form
I've seen every moment in advance before
I've turned my neck a million times

    & written this note
   & been greeted with fire and cheers
I refuse to stop
       —thinking—
   What Perfection has escaped me?

An endless cycle of possibilities clashing in Nothing
with each mistake in the writing inevitable from the beginning
    of time
The doctor's phone number is Pilgrim 1-0000
Are you calling me, Nothing?

The universe be smashed
to smithereens by the oncoming
atomic explosions with
Eisenhower as once President
of a place called U.S.
Gregory wrote the Bomb!
Russians dream of Mars &
when the cosmos goes and
all consciousness after the
final explosion of imagination
in the void it won't have
made any difference that it
all both did and did not
happen, whatever it was once
thought to be so real—
it will be—gone.

O that I might die on the spot
I'll have to go back
any prophecy might have been right
it's all a great Exception

My bus will arrive as foretold
it's the end of another September
war is on the radio ahead
we are all going to the inevitable beauty of doom
a firebox stands sentient before the library
it's hot sun now I'm crazy scribbling
—It began abstract and mindless nowhere
planets of thought have passed
it'll end where it began

I want to return to normal
—but there is no changelessness
but in Nirvana
                    Or is there
Ever Rest, Lord?—and what sages
know and sit.
                    I'm a spy
in Bloomfield on a park bench
        —frightened by buses—

What's that bee doing hanging round my shoe? my borrowed
        and inevitable shoe?
A vast red truck moving with boxes of dead television sets in
        the back

American flag waving over the library

On the bus I sit by a negress

This is an explosion

IV

Back in the same old black hole
    where Possibility closes the
        last door
      and the Great void remains
        . . . a glass
in the dust reflecting the sun,
          fragment of a bottle
    that never knew it existed

               . . . under a tree
that sleeps all winter
      till it grows its eyes
          in May heat
and flowers upward with a thousand
          green sensations
dies, and forgets itself in Snow

    . . . Phantom in Phantom

If we didn't exist, God
would have to create this
to leave no room for complaint
      by any of the birds & bees
who might have missed their
        chance (to be)

    Fate tells a big lie.

      . . . And the big kind Dreamer
is on the nod again
        God sleeps!
He's in for a big surprise
one of his dreams is going to come true
      He'll get the answer too

He'll get the answer too

Just a flash in the cosmic pan
—just an instant when there
            might have been a light
        had there been any pan
                to reflect it—

—we can lie on the bed and imagine
        ourselves away—

I'm afraid to stop breathing—
        first the pain in the
            body
        suffocation, then
            the Death.

V

The pain of gas flowing into the eye
the crooked tooth-drills hanging like gallows
            on a miniature Jupiter
Thru the open window, spring frozen
            in the young tree
the repeated bong of the doorbell
            opening elsewhere
I've come back to the same medicine
        cabinet in the universe—Bong,
I know I'm more real than the dentist!
a serious embarrassment, having grasped to one Self
though admittedly I'd seen it disappear
            over and over

TRACKLESS TRANSIT CORPORATION

runs a bus thru Bloomfield
        . . . blossoming
in the bottom of an unborn daisy
it will vanish into the Whist-not

History will keep repeating
itself forever like the woman
in the image on the Dutch Cleanser box

A way out of the mirror
        was found by the image
that realized its existence
        was only . . .
a stranger completely like myself

A way out for ever! has not been found
to enter the ground whence the images
        rise, and repeat themselves

———————

The sadness is, that every leaf
        has fallen before—

At my feet an ant crawling
        in the broken asphalt—
and this exact white lollypop stick
        & twig of branch
lain next to that soggy match
        near those few grassblades . . .
and I've sat here and took this note
        before and tried to remember—
and now I do—remember what
I'm writing as I write it down
I know when I'm going to stop
I know when I'm forgetting and
know when I

take a jump and change—
Impossible
to do anything but right now in all
the universe at once—
which Art does, and
the Insight of Laughing Gas?

Ha Ha Ha Ha Ha
and the monk laughs
at the moon—
and everybody 10 miles round
in all directions wonders
why—he's just reminding
them—of what—of
the moon, the old dumb moon
of a million lives.

New York, Fall 1958

Mescaline

Rotting Ginsberg, I stared in the mirror naked today
I noticed the old skull, I'm getting balder
my pate gleams in the kitchen light under thin hair
like the skull of some monk in old catacombs lighted by
a guard with flashlight
followed by a mob of tourists
so there is death
my kitten mews, and looks into the closet
Boito sings on the phonograph tonight his ancient song of
    angels
Antinoüs bust in brown photograph still gazing down from my
    wall
a light burst from God's delicate hand sends down a wooden
    dove to the calm virgin
Beato Angelico's universe
the cat's gone mad and scraowls around the floor

What happens when the death gong hits rotting ginsberg on
    the head
what universe do I enter
death death death death death the cat's at rest
are we ever free of—rotting ginsberg
Then let it decay, thank God I know
thank who
thank who
Thank you, O lord, beyond my eye
the path must lead somewhere

the path
the path
thru the rotting shit dump, thru the Angelico orgies
Beep, emit a burst of babe and begone
perhaps that's the answer, wouldn't know till you had a kid
I dunno, never had a kid never will at the rate I'm going

Yes, I should be good, I should get married
find out what it's all about
but I can't stand these women all over me
smell of Naomi
erk, I'm stuck with this familiar rotting ginsberg
can't stand boys even anymore
can't stand
can't stand
and who wants to get fucked up the ass, really?
Immense seas passing over
the flow of time
and who wants to be famous and sign autographs like a movie
      star

I want to know
I want I want ridiculous *to know to know* WHAT rotting gins-
      berg
I want to know what happens after I rot
because I'm already rotting
my hair's falling out I've got a belly I'm sick of sex
my ass drags in the universe I know too much
and not enough
I want to know what happens after I die
well I'll find out soon enough
do I really need to know now?
is that any use at all use use use
death death death death death
god god god god god god god the Lone Ranger
the rhythm of the typewriter

What can I do to Heaven by pounding on Typewriter
I'm stuck change the record Gregory ah excellent he's doing
    just that
and I am too conscious of a million ears
at present creepy ears, making commerce
too many pictures in the newspapers
faded yellowed press clippings
I'm going away from the poem to be a drak contemplative

trash of the mind
trash of the world
man is half trash
all trash in the grave

What can Williams be thinking in Paterson, death so much on
    him
so soon so soon
Williams, what is death?
Do you face the great question now each moment
or do you forget at breakfast looking at your old ugly love in
    the face
are you prepared to be reborn
to give release to this world to enter a heaven
or give release, give release
and all be done—and see a lifetime—all eternity—gone over
into naught, a trick question proposed by the moon to the
    answerless earth
No Glory for man! No Glory for man! No glory for me!
    No me!

No point writing when the spirit doth not lead

New York, 1959

Lysergic Acid

It is a multiple million eyed monster
it is hidden in all its elephants and selves
it hummeth in the electric typewriter
it is electricity connected to itself, if it hath wires
it is a vast Spiderweb
and I am on the last millionth infinite tentacle of the spiderweb,
     a worrier
lost, separated, a worm, a thought, a self
one of the millions of skeletons of China
one of the particular mistakes
I allen Ginsberg a separate consciousness
I who want to be God
I who want to hear the infinite minutest vibration of eternal
     harmony
I who wait trembling my destruction by that aethereal music
     in the fire
I who hate God and give him a name
I who make mistakes on the eternal typewriter
I who am Doomed

But at the far end of the universe the million eyed Spyder that
     hath no name
spinneth of itself endlessly
the monster that is no monster approaches with apples, per-
     fume, railroads, television, skulls
a universe that eats and drinks itself
blood from my skull

Tibetan creature with hairy breast and Zodiac on my stomach
this sacrificial victim unable to have a good time

My face in the mirror, thin hair, blood congested in streaks
      down beneath my eyes, cocksucker, a decay, a talking
      lust
a snaeap, a snarl, a tic of consciousness in infinity
a creep in the eyes of all Universes
trying to escape my Being, unable to pass on to the Eye
I vomit, I am in a trance, my body is seized in convulsion, my
      stomach crawls, water from my mouth, I am here in
      Inferno
dry bones of myriad lifeless mummies naked on the web, the
      Ghosts, I am a Ghost
I cry out where I am in the music, to the room, to whomever
      near, you, Are you God?
No, do you want me to be God?
Is there no Answer?
Must there always be an Answer? you reply,
and were it up to me to say Yes or No—
Thank God I am not God! Thank God I am not God!
But that I long for a Yes of Harmony to penetrate
to every corner of the universe, under every condition what-
      soever
a Yes there Is . . . a Yes I Am . . . a Yes You Are . . . a We

A We
and that must be an It, and a They, and a Thing with No
      Answer
It creepeth, it waiteth, it is still, it is begun, it is the Horns of
      Battle it is Multiple Sclerosis
it is not my hope
it is not my death at Eternity
it is not my word, not poetry
beware my Word

It is a Ghost Trap, woven by priest in Sikkim or Tibet
a crossframe on which a thousand threads of differing color
are strung, a spiritual tennis racket
in which when I look I see aethereal lightwaves radiate
bright energy passing round on the threads as for billions of
      years
the thread-bands magically changing hues one transformed to
      another as if the
Ghost Trap
were an image of the Universe in miniature
conscious sentient part of the interrelated machine.
making waves outward in Time to the Beholder
displaying its own image in miniature once for all
repeated minutely downward with endless variations through-
      out all of itself
it being all the same in every part

This image or energy which reproduces itself at the depths of
      space from the very Beginning
in what might be an O or an Aum
and trailing variations made of the same Word circles round
      itself in the same pattern as its original Appearance
creating a larger Image of itself throughout depths of Time
outward circling thru bands of faroff Nebulae & vast Astrologies
contained, to be true to itself, in a Mandala painted on an
      Elephant's hide,
or in a photograph of a painting on the side of an imaginary
      Elephant which smiles, the how the Elephant looks is an
      irrelevant joke—
it might be a Sign held by a Flaming Demon, or Ogre of Tran-
      science,
or in a photograph of my own belly in the void
or in my eye
or in the eye of the monk who made the Sign
or in its own Eye that stares on Itself at last and dies

and tho an eye can die
and tho my eye can die
the billion-eyed monster, the Nameless, the Answerless, the
    Hidden-from-me, the endless Being
one creature that gives birth to itself
thrills in its minutest particular, sees out of all eyes differently
    at once
One and not One moves on its own ways
I cannot follow

And I have made an image of the monster here
and I will make another
it feels like Cryptozooids
it creeps and undulates beneath the sea
it is coming to take over the city
it invades beneath every Consciousness
it is delicate as the Universe
it makes me vomit
because I am afraid I will miss its appearance
it appears anyway
it appears anyway in the mirror
it washes out of the mirror like the sea
it is myriad undulations
it washes out of the mirror and drowns the beholder
it drowns the world when it drowns the world
it drowns in itself
it floats outward like a corpse filled with music
the noise of war in its head
a babe laugh in its belly
a scream of agony in the dark sea
a smile on the lips of a blind statue
it was there
it was not mine
I wanted to use it for myself
to be heroic
but it is not for sale to this consciousness

it goes its own way forever
it will complete all creatures
it will be the radio of the future
it will hear itself in time
it wants a rest
it is tired of hearing and seeing itself
it wants another form another victim
it wants me
it gives me good reason
it gives me reason to exist
it gives me endless answers
a consciousness to be separate and a consciousness to see
I am beckoned to be One or the other, to say I am both and be
     neither
it can take care of itself without me
it is Both Answerless (it answers not to that name)
it hummeth on the electric typewriter
it types a fragmentary word which is
a fragmentary word,

MANDALA

Gods dance on their own bodies
New flowers open forgetting Death
Celestial eyes beyond the heartbreak of illusion
I see the gay Creator
Bands rise up in anthem to the worlds
Flags and banners waving in transcendence
One image in the end remains myriad-eyed in Eternity
This is the Work! This is the Knowledge! This is the End of
     man!

Palo Alto, June 2, 1959

Magic Psalm

Because this world is on the wing and what cometh no man
    can know
O Phantom that my mind pursues from year to year descend
    from heaven to this shaking flesh
catch up my fleeting eye in the vast Ray that knows no
    bounds—Inseparable—Master—
Giant outside Time with all its falling leaves—Genius of the
    Universe—Magician in Nothingness where appear red
    clouds—
Unspeakable King of the roads that are gone—Unintelligible
    Horse riding out of the graveyard—Sunset spread over
    Cordillera and insect—Gnarl Moth—
Griever—Laugh with no mouth, Heart that never had flesh to
    die—Promise that was not made—Reliever, whose blood
    burns in a million animals wounded—
O Mercy, Destroyer of the World, O Mercy, Creator of Breasted
    Illusions, O Mercy, cacophanous warmouthed doveling,
    Come,
invade my body with the sex of God, choke up my nostrils
    with corruption's infinite caress,
transfigure me to slimy worms of pure sensate transcendency
    I'm still alive,
croak my voice with uglier than reality, a psychic tomato
    speaking Thy million mouths,
Myriad-tongued my Soul, Monster or Angel, Lover that comes
    to fuck me forever—white gown on the Eyeless Squid—
Asshole of the Universe into which I disappear—Elastic Hand

that spoke to Crane—Music that passes into the phono-
graph of years from another Millennium—Ear of the
buildings of NY—

That which I believe—have seen—seek endlessly in leaf dog
eye—fault always, lack—which makes me think—

Desire that created me, Desire I hide in my body, Desire all
Man know Death, Desire surpassing the Babylonian
possible world

that makes my flesh shake orgasm of Thy Name which I don't
know never will never speak—

Speak to Mankind to say the great bell tolls a golden tone on
iron balconies in every million universe,

I am Thy prophet come home this world to scream an unbear-
able Name thru my 5 senses hideous sixth

that knows Thy Hand on its invisible phallus, covered with
electric bulbs of death—

Peace, Resolver where I mess up illusion, Softmouth Vagina
that enters my brain from above, Ark-Dove with a bough
of Death.

Drive me crazy, God I'm ready for disintegration of my mind,
disgrace me in the eye of the earth,

attack my hairy heart with terror eat my cock Invisible croak
of deathfrog leap on me pack of heavy dogs salivating
light,

devour my brain One flow of endless consciousness, I'm scared
of your promise must make scream my prayer in fear—

Descend O Light Creator & Eater of Mankind, disrupt the
world in its madness of bombs and murder,

Volcanos of flesh over London, on Paris a rain of eyes—truck-
loads of angelhearts besmearing Kremlin walls—the
skullcup of light to New York—

myriad jewelled feet on the terraces of Pekin—veils of elec-
trical gas descending over India—cities of Bacteria
invading the brain—the Soul escaping into the rubber
waving mouths of Paradise—

This is the Great Call, this is the Tocsin of the Eternal War, this
is the cry of Mind slain in Nebulae,

this is the Golden Bell of the Church that has never existed,
this is the Boom in the heart of the sunbeam, this is the
trumpet of the Worm at Death,

Appeal of the handless castrate grab Alm golden seed of Futu-
rity thru the quake & volcan of the world—

Shovel my feet under the Andes, splatter my brains on the
Sphinx, drape my beard and hair over Empire State
Building,

cover my belly with hands of moss, fill up my ears with your
lightning, blind me with prophetic rainbows

That I taste the shit of Being at last, that I touch Thy genitals
in the palmtree,

that the vast Ray of Futurity enter my mouth to sound Thy
Creation Forever Unborn, O Beauty invisible to my
Century!

that my prayer surpass my understanding, that I lay my vanity
at Thy foot, that I no longer fear Judgement over Allen
of this world

born in Newark come into Eternity in New York crying again
in Peru for human Tongue to psalm the Unspeakable,

that I surpass desire for transcendency and enter the calm
water of the universe

that I ride out this wave, not drown forever in the flood of my
imagination

that I not be slain thru my own insane magic, this crime be
punished in merciful jails of Death,

men understand my speech out of their own Turkish heart,
the prophets aid me with Proclamation,

the Seraphim acclaim Thy Name, Thyself at once in one huge
Mouth of Universe make meat reply.

June 1960

The Reply

God answers with my doom! I am annulled
　　　　　this poetry blanked from the fiery ledger
　my lies be answered by the worm at my ear
　my visions by the hand falling over my eyes to cover them
　　　　　from sight of my skeleton
　my longing to be God by the trembling bearded jaw flesh
　　　　　that covers my skull like monster-skin
　　Stomach vomiting out the soul-vine, cadaver on
　　　the floor of a bamboo hut, body-meat crawling toward
　　　its fate nightmare rising in my brain
The noise of the drone of creation adoring its Slayer, the yowp
　　　　　of birds to the Infinite, dogbarks like the sound
　of vomit in the air, frogs croaking Death at trees
I am a Seraph and I know not whither I go into the Void
I am a man and I know not whither I go into Death——
　　　　　　　　Christ Christ poor hopeless
　　　　lifted on the Cross between Dimension—
　　　　to see the Ever-Unknowable!
a dead gong shivers thru all flesh and a vast Being enters my
　　　brain from afar that lives forever
　None but the Presence too mighty to record! the Presence
　　in Death, before whom I am helpless
　　　　makes me change from Allen to a skull
Old One-Eye of dreams in which I do not wake but die—
　　　hands pulled into the darkness by a frightful Hand
　　　　　—the worm's blind wriggle, cut—the plough
　　　　　is God himself

What ball of monster darkness from before the universe
    come back to visit me with blind command!
        and I can blank out this consciousness, escape back
           to New York love, and will
        Poor pitiable Christ afraid of the foretold Cross,
           Never to die—
    Escape, but not forever—the Presence will come, the hour
        will come, a strange truth enter the universe, death
           show its Being as before
and I'll despair that *I forgot! forgot!* my fate return,
        tho die of it—
What's sacred when the Thing is all the universe?
    creeps to every soul like a vampire-organ singing behind
        moonlit clouds—
                        poor being come squat
    under bearded stars in a dark field in Peru
        to drop my load—I'll die in horror that I die!
Not dams or pyramids but death, and we to prepare for that
    nakedness, poor bones sucked dry by His long mouth
        of ants and wind, & our souls murdered to prepare
           His Perfection!
The moment's come, He's made His will revealed forever
    and no flight into old Being further than the stars will not
        find terminal in the same dark swaying port
           of unbearable music
No refuge in Myself, which is on fire
    or in the World which is His also to bomb & Devour!
        Recognise His might! Loose hold
    of my hands—my frightened skull
        —for I had chose self-love—
    my eyes, my nose, my face, my cock, my soul—and now
        the faceless Destroyer!
    A billion doors to the same new Being!
The universe turns inside out to devour me!
and the mighty burst of music comes from out the inhuman
           door—

            June 1960

The End

I am I, old Father Fisheye that begat the ocean, the worm at my
    own ear, the serpent turning around a tree,
I sit in the mind of the oak and hide in the rose, I know if any
    wake up, none but my death,
come to me bodies, come to me prophecies, come all fore-
    boding, come spirits and visions,
I receive all, I'll die of cancer, I enter the coffin forever, I close
    my eye, I disappear,
I fall on myself in winter snow, I roll in a great wheel through
    rain, I watch fuckers in convulsion,
car screech, furies groaning their basso music, memory fading
    in the brain, men imitating dogs,
I delight in a woman's belly, youth stretching his breasts and
    thighs to sex, the cock sprung inward
gassing its seed on the lips of Yin, the beasts dance in Siam,
    they sing opera in Moscow,
my boys yearn at dusk on stoops, I enter New York, I play my
    jazz on a Chicago Harpsichord,
Love that bore me I bear back to my Origin with no loss, I float
    over the vomiter
thrilled with my deathlessness, thrilled with this endlessness I
    dice and bury,
come Poet shut up eat my word, and taste my mouth in your
    ear.

New York, 1960

Frontmatter from Original Editions

Original Dedication to *Howl And Other Poems*:

To—

Jack Kerouac, new Buddha of American prose, who spit forth intelligence into eleven books written in half the number of years (1951–1956) – *On the Road, Visions of Neal, Dr Sax, Springtime Mary, The Subterraneans, San Francisco Blues, Some of the Dharma, Book of Dreams, Wake Up, Mexico City Blues,* and *Visions of Gerard* – creating a spontaneous bop prosody and original classic literature. Several phrases and the title of *Howl* are taken from him.

William Seward Burroughs, author of *Naked Lunch*, an endless novel which will drive everybody mad.

Neal Cassady, author of *The First Third*, an autobiography (1949) which enlightened Buddha.

All these books are published in Heaven.

Original Dedication to *Kaddish and Other Poems*:

Dedicated
to Peter Orlovsky
in
Paradise

'Taste my mouth in your ear'

Original epigraph from *Howl And Other Poems*:

'Unscrew the locks from the doors!
Unscrew the doors themselves from their jambs!'

Original epigraph from *Kaddish and Other Poems*:

'– Die,
If thou wouldst be with that which thou dost seek!'

Original author notes from *Kaddish and Other Poems*:

'Magic Psalm', 'The Reply' and 'The End' record visions experienced after drinking Ayahuasca, an Amazon spiritual potion. The message is: Widen the area of consciousness. – A. G.

Acknowledged, the established literary quarterlies of my day are bankrupt poetically thru their own hatred, dull ambition or loud-mouthed obtuseness. These poems were printed in *Yugen, Combustion, Liberation, Beatitude, Playboy, Big Table, Evergreen Review, Jargon 31, New Directions 17, The Outsider, New Departures, Jabberwock (Sidewalk), Poetry London-NY* and strangely the London *Times Literary Supplement*. Most of these publications started in the last half-decade, two were begun by youths who quit editing university magazines to avoid academic censorship.

– A. G. (Dated 1961)

Contemporary ... Provocative ... Outrageous ...
Prophetic ... Groundbreaking ... Funny ... Disturbing ...
Different ... Moving ... Revolutionary ... Inspiring ...
Subversive ... Life-changing ...

What makes a modern classic?

At Penguin Classics our mission has always been to make the best books ever written available to everyone. And that also means constantly redefining and refreshing exactly what makes a 'classic'. That's where Modern Classics come in. Since 1961 they have been an organic, ever-growing and ever-evolving list of books from the last hundred (or so) years that we believe will continue to be read over and over again.

They could be books that have inspired political dissent, such as *Animal Farm*. Some, like *Lolita* or *A Clockwork Orange*, may have caused shock and outrage. Many have led to great films, from *In Cold Blood* to *One Flew Over the Cuckoo's Nest*. They have broken down barriers – whether social, sexual, or, in the case of *Ulysses*, the boundaries of language itself. And they might – like *Goldfinger* or *Scoop* – just be pure classic escapism. Whatever the reason, Penguin Modern Classics continue to inspire, entertain and enlighten millions of readers everywhere.

'No publisher has had more influence on reading habits than Penguin'
Independent

'Penguins provided a crash course in world literature'
Guardian

The best books ever written

PENGUIN 🐧 CLASSICS

SINCE 1946

Find out more at www.penguinclassics.com